DIVERSITY

First published in 2020 by the University of Sydney

Funded by the University of Sydney Faculty of Arts and Social Sciences, School of Literature, Art and Media

Sydney University Press
Fisher Library F03
University of Sydney
NSW 2006 AUSTRALIA

Email: sup.info@sydney.edu.au
sydneyuniversitypress.com.au

A catalogue record for this book is available from the National Library of Australia

ISBN: 978-1-74210-446-1 (paperback)
ISBN: 978-1-74210-447-8 (epub)
ISBN: 978-1-74210-448-5 (mobi)

CONTENTS

ACKNOWLEDGEMENTS ix
FOREWORD xi

KING ST: LESBIANISM 3
Lou Garcia-Dolnik

DINNER TABLE, 2019 5
Amy Wang

INTOLERANT 7
Sheree Strange

BLACK PROTEST 25
Harold Legaspi

THROWING GLITTER AT CHRISTIANS 27
Connor Parissis

NIGHTCLUBBING 35
Harold Legaspi

GONE BOY 36
Harold Legaspi

KYLIE 39
Adelia Croser

THE FIRST SATURDAY IN MARCH 57
John Hannaford

THE SHAME OF PRIVILEGE 65
James Mukheibir

EMBODIMENT 75
Anastasia Taig

WHEN A KISS IS A QUEER, UNCERTAIN THING 77
Amy Wang

STRANGER IN DELHI 79
Grace Jing Johnson

TWINS 95
Anastasia Taig

PARALYSIS 97
Anastasia Taig

STORIES BEHIND OPERA CURATION 100
Jing Cai

ANYWHERE, EVERYWHERE 107
Sarah Poh

ECOTONE 110
Sofia Ahmad

A PARADOX OF SEA AND COAL 112
Gabrielle Cadenhead

DIVERSITY? NOT SO MUCH HERE 114
Cherita Zhu

مُحَمّدْ رياض عَوَاد 119
Mohammad Awad

ASSIMILATION 121
Mary Stanley

COLOURED RAINDROPS 144
Bethany Carter

FUN-SIZED DIVERSITY 146
Mohammad Awad

I'M SORRY 153
Zhipei Zheng

HINDI/ENGLISH INDIAN 156
Rhea L Nath

ENOUGH 158
Raz Badiyan

HIGH COUNTRY 159
Scott Whittingham

THE LEAVES TURN BROWN IN SUMMER 161
Hannah Roux

MOONLIGHT MOTEL 163
Ivy Waters

I THINK OF CLOTHES IN PERSONAL LATIN 174
Misbah Ansari

PRESSURE 176
Sarah Carol Hughes

BURNING THE MASKS 177
Anastasia Taig

FILTHY RICH 178
Harold Legaspi

DINNER IN THE UNDERGROUND 190
Elizabeth Wheeler

AS FIRE TO SNOW 198
Rosie Mulray

MOTHER EARTH 201
Scott Whittingham

DIVERSITY AND GENDER IN THE COMPOSITIONAL RELATIONSHIP OF ROBERT AND CLARA SCHUMANN 203
Katarina Grobler

THE MULTI-COLOURED ROAD TO AUSTRALIA 226
Vrishali Jain

IRAN 238
Raz Badiyan

STARRY NIGHT 239
Naosheyrvaan Nasir

TREE OF LIFE 240
Scott Whittingham

REMEMBERING EUNICE 242
Gabrielle Cadenhead

PLANT AND ANIMAL 244
Elizabeth Mora

ABOUT THE CONTRIBUTORS 255
ABOUT THE EDITORS 271

IMAGES

AARHUS PRIDE #1 179
Djuna Hallsworth

AARHUS PRIDE #2 180
Djuna Hallsworth

AARHUS PRIDE #3 181
Djuna Hallsworth

COLOURISM 182
Yasodara S. B. W. Puhule-Gamayalage

GENETIC DIVERSITY 183
Scott Whittingham

OAK TREE 184
Memi Adams

PINE TREE 185
Memi Adams

BEYOND RELIGION AND DIVERSITY 186
Scott Whittingham

BANKSIA 187
Scott Whittingham

ELLE EST L'UNIVERS 1 188
Keesha Field

ELLE EST L'UNIVERS 3 189
Keesha Field

ACKNOWLEDGEMENTS

It has been a long and difficult, though rewarding, journey to publish this anthology. There are so many people to thank, who have all had a part in turning our ideas into a published work.

First of all we would like to specifically thank Agata Mrva-Montoya. We are extremely grateful for your support and guidance throughout this project. You have taught us more than we could learn in any classroom, and we all appreciate the advice you've given as well as your belief in us.

Thank you to Maeve Marsden. We are grateful for your contribution to this year's anthology, and for sharing your own thoughts on diversity.

To the artists, photographers and writers who contributed to this year's anthology, we could not have created this book without you. You have each brought a unique and moving voice to the theme of diversity. We set out to curate a collection of ideas and experiences that deserved to be heard, and we hope that everyone is as inspired by each story and artwork as we are.

Thank you to the academic liaison librarians for your support in promoting the anthology to the student community. Thank you to SUPRA for your legal advice and for helping us to protect our authors. Thank you to Teresa Ornelas for your dedication to marketing the anthology and giving your time to write for our blog.

And lastly, to the anthology team. I could not have asked for a better group of people to do this with. Every single one of you has put endless hours into this project to make it happen. From the countless posters you've put up all over campus, to the time you've all put into editing every single submission. You have all worked extremely hard and I hope you are as proud of it as I am.

FOREWORD

Maeve Marsden

I have always told stories, though in truth I have not always been a writer, prone instead to insisting people listened as I improvised my way through another great, narrative adventure. Today, I might claim to being more pint-sized spoken word artist than a rather precocious child – that I was shaping an oral history of sorts; but I'm not sure retroactively lending creative weight to my extroversion is quite fair. I blame my verbosity on being raised with too much love and attention – my mothers were so devoted as to spoil us, inspired both by love and a fervent desire to disprove homophobic notions of family. I was raised with a love of books and writing – one mother a librarian, the other an avid reader – as well as a righteous passion for educating the masses about queer families, one over-share at a time. Perhaps I learned to tell my own story to counter discrimination, or perhaps there's just a sort of showmanship built into my DNA. Nature/nurture, chicken/egg, top/bottom, who can say?

Well into adulthood, I touted my otherness as having value. I was useful to the world because I was different and I could demonstrate the value of 'diverse' families by my demonstrable success as a human being. It took time, reading, listening to thinkers bigger than I, to realise the shortcomings of my approach. An individual is not diverse, neither grammatically nor anthropologically; diversity requires a variety of experiences. In the end, my work only really started to resonate when I devoted my precocious enthusiasm towards the sharing of multiple queer narratives, not just my own. Now, through the national storytelling project I curate *Queerstories*, I am known not for telling my own story but for providing a platform where others tell theirs.

I have to admit to a certain cringe I experience when *Queerstories* is praised for its diversity, not because I am not proud of the project, but because I worry that people aren't actually listening to the stories, instead scrolling through lists of identity categories in their head. I worry that work described as 'diverse' is considered worthy rather than good.

If I am honest, this cringe gave me pause when I was invited to write a foreword for a 'diversity' themed anthology, afraid I would be reading work about diversity rather than a diverse collection of work. You can imagine my relief and delight then, to read a collection truly diverse in style, content, form and ideas. Discussions of marginalised identities feature, countering the dominant narratives most of these authors would have grown up with, but broadly speaking herein is a collection of writers offered the freedom to explore the specificity of their experience, without having to cater to a mainstream gaze.

In many sectors, 'diversity and inclusion' have become buzzwords divorced from their meaning, a KPI on countless corporate agendas. For those committed to writing and publishing, I think the word has more use as a guiding principle for creativity than an end goal. Diversity isn't a task achieved but rather the ongoing desire for encountering and celebrating new ideas and narratives, for multiplicity, for a collective. Perhaps it's best to think of 'diversity' as being inherent to curiosity, that foundational element of what it means to be a writer. A curious mind seeks new fascinations – a curious mind should want more than what it has previously been offered.

At a time when the arts and literature are criminally underfunded, in a country governed by leaders who value assimilation over multiplicity, nurturing a voracious appetite for stories that challenge our worldview is essential. While I still have a twinge of uncertainty about the value of the buzzword 'diversity', I am heartened by the fact a group of students engaged in the craft of storytelling have published such a collection, that this generation of writers, editors and publishers understands the deep importance of complex, engaging and, yes, diverse stories about the world in which we live.

DIVERSITY

KING ST: LESBIANISM

Lou Garcia-Dolnik

It liked to lick tar
from its own durried dustbins and
use the exhaust to wipe the day,

washing the dirt from its black and white

& spluttered all red and expulsive
in the course of its own performance.

everything in the picture stirring
with photographic buzz
            glances cutting through it
and hashtags fashioned in the expected way,

many families in parks and cafes, as in

'you stupid kite/get out of that tree!' or
you stupid dyke.

no hour to figure anything out

aware that left and right
so many men
straight parade engulfing everything,

I kissed her

and didn't it genuflect for that wokeness?
hoping it could get anywhere
with the rainbow alphabet

a smoke dirge
in middle distance:

thank you, thank you
for your lesbianism. Thank-

DINNER TABLE, 2019

Amy Wang

& there we sit. perfect
circular table spin-stopping (we,
like a half-built thing
bleeding on a pottery wheel).
엄마 says stop
shaking my legs,
& i shake
a little quieter. our voices are loud
but our hearts whisper
in three foreign tongues.
the chopsticks (& something else that looks like heavy palms,
sounds like a kneeled prayer,
tastes like sacrifice)
bind us. & we,
none of us are home here
but we still build houses with all this blood.
姑妈 speaks English like a mosaic.

if we have taught each other anything,
it is how to endure (even this) into art.

(엄마 = mum [Korean]; 姑妈 = paternal aunt [Chinese])

INTOLERANT

Sheree Strange

Thai Take-away – Glebe

This is the only place in the world I feel comfortable ordering the spring rolls. I love spring rolls, but even when a menu promises me that they're gluten-free, they're invariably made with soy sauce, or served with soy sauce, or fried in oil that's cross-contaminated. Not many people realise that soy sauce contains wheat or that gluten proteins can leech out into cooking oil. I've even tried making my own wheat-free spring rolls, but I failed dismally. I've been ordering them here for years and I've never had a problem. They taste even better for being able to relish the freedom; I feel it in the crisp crunch and see it in the flakes that dust down my jumper.

I order other things as well. There's an entire A3 page of vegetarian options, but I always go for the duck and the pork belly. I figure I've given up enough and I devour any and all meats without compunction.

There are signs everywhere in this tiny, cramped kitchen that say 'Cash Only'. Normally, I'd object to such blatant millennial discriminatory policies and poorly disguised tax evasion, but there's a Big Four ATM just a few doors down and I want the spring rolls, so I make an exception. They make the food fresh, and you can watch them, if you like, perched on one of their mismatched plastic stools. It's like going to the theatre; they shout, and twist, and flip, and chop, and cast and cry out, 'Order 47!' Someone else scurries forth to collect their two containers, and I marvel at their restraint. I never walk out with fewer than four.

Sometimes, when it's too cold or dark outside, or I'm just feeling particularly indulgent, I'll order delivery through EatNow. The owner walks it over himself instead of summoning a driver to carry my meal(s) around the corner. I always order enough to feed a small army, telling myself that I'll have the leftovers for lunch over the next few days, even though I know that it's never as good reheated.

Spanish Tapas – Glebe

I watch enviously as the couple at the next table devour their half-price pizza. Maybe they got one of the bottomless deals, because the waiters keep bringing over more. The woman laughs and nods as the man mumbles something through a mouthful of crust and mozzarella.

My dining companions wanted to order the pizza too, but they changed their minds after my friend jerked her head towards me with pitying eyes. That prompted the strangers at the table to ask the question. It's always awkward when someone asks me over dinner why I'm eating something different. No matter how I answer them, my explanation is followed by more questions. They want to know if I'm 'real' or 'fake' gluten-free. They want to know what happens to my body when I'm exposed to gluten accidentally. That's how I end up talking about my lower intestine over appetisers. Even if I try to change the subject, they'll persist until I explain exactly how my skin becomes inflamed and sore, my stomach rejects anything solid for days, and my mind becomes a Dickensian fog. They tell me I must miss breads and pastas, and I tell them honestly that I don't, but I do miss peanut M&Ms so much that it brings me to tears when I'm pre-menstrual. They ask me if I'm ever tempted to have a blow-out one day and eat as much gluten as I can, and I tell them no. They shake their heads disbelievingly and one woman says vehemently that she could never give up bread. I sip my drink, and smile, as though I've never heard it before.

The live flamenco show starts, and it's perfectly loud and audacious enough that all attention is appropriately deflected from my dietary requirements. The bread-lover is pulled up to dance with them and she takes her glass of sangria with her. We all cheer enthusiastically as she twirls.

When the waiter comes, he has to shout to make himself heard. I want to order the *Tortilla de Espinaca*, but I don't know how to pronounce it, and I'm sure if I try the music will stop just in time for everyone to hear me fuck it up. I ask for the Spanish

Olives instead, and another Cosmopolitan (because they're only twelve bucks here, so I can afford two). The waiter smiles and the rest of the table orders food and drinks in turn. The woman next to me asks for *Huevos a la Flamenca* without blinking, and a beer. Her order arrives long before mine.

Craft Beer and Pub Food – The Rocks

I didn't realise we'd have to climb a hill to reach this place, stepping carefully in the footholds of old concrete stairs on a steep incline, so we all arrive a little out of breath. The men have pulled off their suit jackets and slung them over their shoulders, and I can see small patches of perspiration soaked through their neatly pressed white and light blue shirts. 'I'm ready for a beer,' one of them says, and we all groan appreciatively, even me.

Taking a table outside in the shade, they debate their selections endlessly. They've decided to get a few tasting paddles, wooden blocks with round holes for specially designed small glasses containing a personally curated variety of craft beers. My mouth is dry, and I could have secured a vodka soda and finished it in the time it takes them to narrow down their top ten, but I'm trying to be polite. I don't ask about gluten-free beer options; a quenching brew would be wonderful, of course, but I'm trying not to draw attention to myself. No one notices until the waitress returns with three paddles and a single shot glass of clear liquid, with two lime wedges on the rim, for me. 'Ah, shit,' my boss says. 'Forgot you can't have beer.' I tell him not to worry about it and take a grateful gulp as they set about figuring out which beer is which.

They ask for menus and I order another drink. We're all quiet for a minute, as they study the six varieties of burger, and I read with interest about the history of the building. I pull out one of the lime wedges to suck. When the waitress returns with a pen and a notepad, they all list their demands: medium rare, extra cheese, chips instead of salad, no tomato, no pickles, extra pickles and two plates of chicken wings for the table. When they turn to me, I ask for another vodka soda, and my boss starts shouting.

It's a good-natured admonishment, but an admonishment nonetheless. 'You picked the bloody place!' he yells. 'Why didn't you pick somewhere you could eat?'

I try to smile apologetically at the waitress, but she doesn't notice, because he rounds on her, 'Can you get the chef to make something gluten-free for her?'

The waitress nods, and darts back to the safety of the kitchen. He shakes his head, and none of the others will meet my eye. One of them says something about a typo in the meeting minutes that turned a comment about KPIs into something quite profane, and everybody laughs, breaking the tension.

When the waitress returns, holding two wide platters of steaming wings coated in a reddish sauce, she says brightly, 'The chef says these are gluten-free!' Looking at me, she adds, 'Let me know if you want more.'

I'm not even hungry. I ate before we left the office, in anticipation of an evening of lime wedges. But now they're all staring at me, so I reach forward and retrieve a wing. There's no way to eat chicken wings without making a mess. No matter how many serviettes you use, there will always be a smear of tell-tale sauce on your chin, on your little finger, on your elbow, revealing your indulgence to every passerby on the way home. I place the bones on my empty bread plate and reach for another. No one else is touching them now that they're 'safe' for me to eat. I plead with my eyes, for the colleague sitting across from me to take one. Eventually, he does, and I exhale. I leave the second wing half-eaten, next to the remnants of the first.

When the burgers arrive, they all tuck in, and enthuse about the umami flavour of the marbled meat, the softness of the bun, the smokiness of the bacon. The man on my left reaches forward and dips three of his chips in the saucy wings platter.

'You fucking idiot!' our boss declares, revealing to all a half-masticated mouthful of his meal. 'She can't eat them now!' He points to me, with a greasy finger.

It's fine, it's fine; I mouth the words, but I don't bother saying them. Everyone is shouting, and no one will hear me anyway.

Dine-In Sushi – CBD

My mother-in-law is in town, and she asks my husband to choose a place for us all to have an early dinner. It's only about 5:30 pm when we meet. We try to hug and say hello on the corner of York

Street, like oblivious rocks in a stream of suited commuters. My husband knows where we're going, so he takes the lead, telling us over his shoulder that he chose the Japanese place with the best ratings on TripAdvisor. My mother-in-law looks at me questioningly. I nod to reassure her. I tell her that I love sushi. Sashimi makes my stomach churn, ever since I ate some in a moment of desperation at an airport and wound up vomiting in the tiny airplane bathroom mid-flight, but I love everything else. In fact, my mouth starts to water as I think about delicious seaweed-wrapped rolls with fluffy, sticky rice, and a generous smear of wasabi.

When we arrive, we're the first diners and we have our pick of the tables. The waiter is friendly, but quiet, and he brings us chilled water straight away. My husband clears his throat and loudly says that I have a dietary requirement and asks him to explain which items on the menu are gluten-free. The waiter hasn't even put the water down yet, and he looks confused. I want to hush my husband, tell him to give the guy a moment, but the genie is already out of the bottle.

In the end, it takes us fifteen minutes and many useless hand gestures to explain gluten to the waiter. He asks us to Google Translate the word for him on his Samsung phone. When he looks at the equivalent character, his face falls, and he runs to the kitchen. When he comes back, he says only, 'Sashimi for you!'

I point to the cooked tuna and vegetarian delight rolls on the menu, 'What about these? Surely –'

He shakes his head, vigorously. 'No, no. Only sashimi.'

I don't quite believe him, but I don't dare contradict him. I have an operations meeting at work the next day, and they're trying under the best of circumstances. I can't show up bloated and sick and unable to follow what's being said around me. My mother-in-law's eyes are narrowed, she's shooting daggers at my husband, and he looks like a puppy dog that can't find his bone. She suggests leaving immediately, finding someplace else, but I insist that it's fine. It's fine. I order a glass of sauvignon blanc and decline the sashimi. The waiter brings over a small bowl of grapes, gratis, and gives me an apologetic smile.

I try to distract my mother-in-law from the now very audible rumbles of my stomach as they tuck into towering plates of rolls and rice. I ask her about her work, but I don't know anything about property law or conveyancing, so the conversation doesn't last for long. My husband jumps in to tell her about his idea for a blog, and I order another glass of wine.

I'm starving by the time we leave. Once we've hugged my mother-in-law goodbye, my husband suggests we find somewhere else to get something I can eat. I tell him not to worry about it; I know there are leftovers in the fridge at home.

Indian Cuisine – Glebe

My family loves this place. Whenever my parents come to town, my father insists that we eat here at least once, sometimes twice. I don't mind because it's one of the few restaurants where I feel spoiled for choice. I can eat almost anything, save the naan and samosas, and my husband is happy to eat my share of those. I avoided eating the dosa for years, until my father finally made me ask the waiter about its ingredients. Rice flour, a crisp crêpe stuffed with spicy lamb mince. It crunches when you cut into it and pairs delightfully with a coconut chutney that they serve on the side. I ordered one last time, and held my breath the rest of the meal, nervously examining my skin and probing my mind for any symptoms showing, but I was fine. My father says we should order the dosa again, and I agree enthusiastically.

My husband insists on getting the butter chicken, and I call him a philistine white boy, even though I secretly love its creamy sweetness. I ask for the palak paneer and the lamb korma. My mother says that those three dishes, plus the dosas and the naan, will be enough for all of us. She's right, the serving sizes here are deceptive. What looks like a tiny bowl the size of your fist actually holds three times as much as it appears to, and you only realise that once you're scooping the contents onto your plate.

Once the waiter takes our order – the same one who reassured me last time about the dosa – my mother waits for him to leave, then sneaks a bottle of wine out of her handbag. It's a BYO restaurant, but she still tries to be surreptitious. She'll never admit it, but I think she hopes she'll avoid the corkage charge if she pours the wine herself and they never see her do it. Some people might call that cheap, but she calls it sensible.

Her sensibility strikes again when she asks for a doggy bag

to take home the leftover naan, and objects loudly to the ten cent charge for a container. She insists on wrapping it up in the complimentary serviettes instead, dropping the parcel on top of the now empty wine bottle in her handbag. I roll my eyes and satisfy myself with the knowledge that she'll be cleaning crumbs out of her bag for a month.

The next morning, I make my husband a bacon and egg naan sandwich. I sip a black coffee as he eats it, and he tells me it's better than anything I've ever made with Wonder White.

European Fine Dining – Circular Quay

We've arrived early for dinner with my sister-in-law, and we're staring wide-eyed around the restaurant. My husband looks impressed, and I'm sure I look anxious, because we are both noticeably under-dressed. It's got a casual name, but this is without a doubt the swankiest establishment to which I've ever been granted entry. The website says a 'relaxed, contemporary interior', and I'd imagine it's about as relaxed as Buckingham Palace. I'm wearing jeans, my pair with the waistband held together by a safety pin because the button fell off long ago. I tuck myself under the table, and vow not to stand again until we're leaving.

We're seated outside where it's windy and cold, but the views are spectacular. The waiter, who has a neatly pressed bright white linen cloth draped over his forearm, insists on taking our drink order, even though the rest of our party hasn't arrived. My husband asks for a negroni, I ask for a margarita, and we both cross our fingers that we won't have to pay for them ourselves. When we drink them, we find they're so delicious that they might be worth skipping out on rent this month. The guest of honour arrives, and she orders another round.

I don't mention that I'm gluten-free, but my sister-in-law grills the nice waiter, making sure he double-checks with the kitchen about every single item we order to share. She's so insistent, and I'm so silent, that he mistakes her for the intolerant one. After the mains are cleared, and we're tucking into the most decadent desserts that have ever been placed on plates, he sees her take a bite of the apple tart.

He comes flying across the room, arms outstretched like a superhero. He shouts, 'No! No! Not that one! Not for you!'

I hold my breath and after a beat her confusion gives way to mirth.

When she stops laughing – I'm still not breathing – she apologises to the waiter and explains that I'm the one with the 'problem'. She gestures to me, and his face relaxes. I can feel every drop of hot red blood in my body rush to my cheeks, and I reiterate her apology at least four times. He nods good-naturedly and backs away.

They all carry on like nothing happened, and I wonder if it's possible to disappear through sheer force of will.

Turkish Fast Food – Newtown

It's the end of the night for most people, and options for food are plentiful, far more than they would have been six years ago, before the lockout. Still, they're not plentiful enough to quite guarantee a lining on my own problematic stomach. I'm trying my luck with this place.

I miss falafel. When I was travelling in the Middle East, I could get traditional falafel made only with chickpea flour and fried in oil that touched nothing else. My mouth still waters remembering it now, and once a year or so Facebook flashes up a 'memory' to ensure my nostalgic desire never wanes. I swallow and look to the other side of the board menu behind the counter.

Everyone here is a bit bedraggled, a bit disoriented, a bit ready to jump in an Uber and call it a night, just as soon as they've devoured their kebab with everything. One man in a formerly white t-shirt is slumped over a tiny table, happily chomping away, ignoring the steady stream of sauces and juices running down his forearms into a puddle around his elbows. He has a box of hot chips as well, coated in a heavy snowstorm of chicken salt. I avert my eyes and step forward when the attendant beckons.

I ask him for a kebab plate, with no tabouli. He pulls out a styrofoam tray, and starts loading it past the brim: a heap of recently shaved chicken, two hearty handfuls of generic grated cheese, chopped lettuce, tomato, onion and half a bottle of garlic sauce. He motions for me to tap my card, and I do so without taking my eyes off the food. I can hear my stomach yearning, even over the sighs and moans of the drunks and the steady stream of late-night traffic passing outside.

I'm reaching out for the styrofoam tray, and right as he's about to pass it to me, he leans over with his other hand and grabs a large plain pita from the stack beside the cash register. He throws it right on top.

He shoves down the lid, and smiles. 'Here you go.'

'Thanks,' I say, trying to return his grin.

I take it from him, and walk it out to my friend, who's been waiting patiently on the pavement outside. She stubs out her cigarette.

'Here,' I hold it out to her. 'You have it.'

'You sure?'

'Yeah, I'm sure. I'll eat at home.'

Modern Australian Cuisine – Coogee

It's one of those rare nights that every single one of my in-laws are in the same city at the same time. We meet in Coogee and traipse around for nearly an hour to find a restaurant on which they can all agree. The hostess says it will be a forty-five-minute wait for a table for five, so we retreat to the hotel bar across the street.

We need to fight for a table there too. The room is cavernous, almost empty, and I wonder why they don't just put out more tables and chairs. Perhaps the acres of room become a dance floor when Coogee kicks off on summer Saturdays. And it's loud;

the top forty radio tracks echo, so we have to lean in close to one another to speak. My father-in-law says the lighting is too low for him to read the menu. He pulls out his phone and uses the torch.

I say I'll have a vodka soda, but everyone else wants to order a meat and cheese platter. They've barely eaten all day, they implore me, and they can't possibly wait another thirty-five minutes. I shrug in nonchalant agreement, and my husband points out that they offer gluten-free crackers. I tell him to make sure the prosciutto and chorizo are okay too, when he orders, and he rolls his eyes at me. 'I know the drill,' he says, in long-suffering tones.

When he gets back from the bar, he slides my drink over to me and winks. 'I checked, we're all good!' he says over the music, and I nod.

The fifteen-minute wait for the platter is interminable. We've all finished our drinks, our table will be ready at the other restaurant soon, and it's too difficult, with the noise, to hold a conversation about anything other than how hungry they all are. I wonder, for a second, if my sister-in-law might kiss the waiter when he approaches with the wooden board, because she looks as though she's considering it.

They all swarm upon the sustenance, but I hold back. It looks like they've given us ham instead of chorizo. My husband has noticed, too. He knows the drill, after all.

'Ham's normally fine!' he says. 'And we don't have time to send it back, really.'

He's right. I've never encountered ham with gluten before. And it looks good, fresh pink slices curled around one another in a towering pile. I use the little tongs to place a couple on top of a cracker, and bite in. I marvel at how tasty it is along with everybody else.

I don't notice anything until we're already seated at the next restaurant for dinner. I'm listening to my husband order, and when I reach over to check my phone, I notice that the flesh of my inner arms is tender.

By the time three of our five dishes have arrived, I have to excuse myself to the bathroom. I stumble as I miss the step up into the cubicle. I pull off my bra and shove it into my purse. It's too painful to wear now that my whole rib cage feels deeply bruised.

I make it through the rest of the dinner, struggling to keep my mind clear of fog. I have no idea what I'm saying when I'm asked to contribute to the conversation. Everyone's looking at me with wide-eyed pity, but they let me talk and we all pretend that it's fine. I have to excuse myself to the bathroom twice more, and I trip on the same step every time. I manage to eat about six bites of everything, but I can barely keep them down. When the waitress comes over and asks if we want dessert, I fight back tears, and thankfully everyone declines.

My husband summons an Uber to take us home. I try to ask him, in fumbling sentences, to tell the driver that I'm sick, not drunk. I don't want to trash his customer rating and I know how this must look. I have no idea whether he does or doesn't, because every inch of my skin, every muscle in my body, is screaming. I silently will the contents of my stomach to stay where they are, just until we make it home. We make it.

After I've thrown up as much as it's possible for a human to throw up, I take two Nurofen. My husband makes me a green tea, and I try to thank him, but the words escape me. He tells me he knows what I mean, and goes to pat my shoulder gently, but I shy away from his touch. He doesn't know the drill that well, not well enough to override his instincts to comfort me by touching my aching body. The symptoms last for two days. I sleep, cry, vomit and shit, until the fog clears.

Contemporary Fusion – Newtown

I've combed through the restaurant website a hundred times, ever since they suggested the place, and it looks good. It promises an 'eclectic grazing menu' that caters for all dietary options: vegetarian, vegan, or anything else. I have to reassure all of the attendees about a thousand times each that I'm happy with the venue selection.

I worried, though, when I walked past the place a couple of weeks ago, that one of the attendees – a wheelchair user – might struggle to navigate inside. It looked like the owners had crammed in as many tables as they could, which would normally be a good sign, but it doesn't leave much space to navigate between them. When I arrive the night of the party, I heave a sigh of relief. They've rearranged the room to create widened paths. That's a good start.

I'm the third-last to arrive, and the organiser tells me they've pre-ordered a banquet to serve everybody. I try not to show her my gritted teeth as I smile. Based on past experience there will be one, maybe two, banquet options that I can actually eat. And they're probably salads. I pick up one of the champagne cocktails and turn to hug another person hello. It's fine, I tell myself. I'm not here for the food.

Shortly before the first plates arrive, the two waitresses hand around a little pamphlet, detailing the courses that will be served. It's all tapas-style, a 'fusion of international flavours', and the description of each dish makes my mouth water. My eyes are drawn to the heading. GLUTEN-FREE BANQUET, it says. The font is small, but bold. I blink, take another sip of the cocktail, and look at it again.

'Excuse me,' I say to one of the waitresses as she clears empty glasses from the table. 'Is this – it says it's a gluten-free banquet?'

'That's right,' she says. 'The organiser said you needed gluten-free meals.'

'Is this – it's just for me, right?'

She frowns slightly. 'Um, no? Everyone will be eating the same banquet. Has there been a mistake?'

I start composing, in my head, the scolding I will give the organiser later. There is only one thing worse than eating a sad, lonely salad while everyone else tucks into pastas and curry puffs, and that's subjecting everyone else to the grainy gluten substitutes that you've convinced yourself to love (for lack of any alternatives).

The waitress seems to sense my discomfort. She smiles, and says, 'It's not all that different to our other banquets. Most of our platters are gluten-free anyway. It'll be fine!'

I'm not entirely convinced, but I try to look as though I am.

That night, I eat everything, including my words. Not a single attendee seemed to even notice the absence of bread and soy sauce. Each platter was quickly cleared of seared pork fillet medallions, lemongrass marinated chicken tenderloins, and New York-style crushed chat potatoes.

On my way home, curled up in the back of a cab, trying not to inhale too deeply lest I catch a whiff of the driver's body odour and/or risk popping the safety pin off my jeans, I realise something. It's the first time I've ever been able to eat everything off a banquet menu. I could talk to my fellow party-goers about the flavours and textures of every single dish. No one looked at me with wide, pitying eyes, or apologised for enjoying the garlic bread. This must be what it's like to be normal.

BLACK PROTEST

Harold Legaspi

We all have our histories.
A young black poet,
Fresh off the pages, said to me once:
'Be aggressive ... be very, very aggressive.'
I wondered if his politics
Was his redemption.

As if this was his way to be heard in everyday life,
As if his poetry carried the wisdom of Gods;
To light humanity's trodden path.
As if he had the answers,
A polemic for every day of the week.

To the question:
How dare you.

To Gods:
I believe.

How do we carry on with false promise?
How do we repair the trauma we inherited?
The young black poet will grow wiser,
Inhale his own voice,
Sink to the murk of life.
And I, I will lodge myself like
A fishbone in his throat.

THROWING GLITTER AT CHRISTIANS

Connor Parissis

My face, doused in rage, made the front page of *The Daily Telegraph*. Forced into a spotlight of infamy – a scapegoat for someone else's agenda. 'Yes Campaigners Show Their True Colours,' Miranda Devine wrote, labelling me a 'feral rainbow gremlin'. The Murdoch Press narrative dominated the scene, my voice too small to matter. I was never asked what made me so mad.

The event in question was a protest, mystified by trauma, against the backdrop of Australia's postal survey on marriage equality. Since high school, I had teetered on a tightrope stretched across a cavernous pit of 'faggots' and 'pooftahs.' When the government decided to let the people vote on marriage equality, the homophobes grew braver. Their insults worsened. Their hatred ignited.

'Paedophiles' and 'dog-fuckers' were the insults, among many, that lit the fuse within me that day. For the sake of open dialogue and free expression, these campaigners, behind the masquerade of a religious stall, offered free kebabs with a side of homophobia and fear-mongering. They would have conversations, wary of passerbys like myself. My ears perked intently as I overheard their more heinous statements. I witnessed faces of disgust. Most people who were handed a leaflet were quick to tear it up. As the university's elected 'Queer Officer', students approached me on the bustling avenue, to and from class, to vent their anger at the vitriol these religious groups were spewing.

'Are you hearing this shit?'

'They told me, to my face, that marriage equality will lead to bestiality.'

'When I argued back, they called me a paedophile!'

'This is hate speech! We have to do something!'

Murmurs echoed across the bustling campus. By midday, hundreds joined forces, surrounding the NO campaigners. The procession began with chants: 'Pack up and go home,' and 'Homophobia and transphobia are not welcome here.' Many on the opposite side disappeared in cowardice, afraid of confrontation – they took their views home with them. A select few persevered, holding their placards high above their heads with such valiant rigour.

'Fuck this,' I thought, passing the anchor of a megaphone to the person next to me. I teetered around the periphery of the congregation. The stocky campus security guard watched me intently with necessary suspicion. His reflexes, however, were not as quick as mine. I lunged forward, grasped the placard leaning against the stall and ran as the crowd erupted in cheers and parted the way for my escape.

Snapshots savoured the memory – my first claim to infamy. There is exhilaration in rebellion and I had become thirsty for more.

I returned to the protest shortly after, having discarded the placard in a nearby bush. Tensions still bubbled. Protesters had taken to the megaphone denouncing the NO campaigners for their fallacies. They yelled with such passion – the pain of the vote a scar on all of us. Yet valiant the opposition remained, signs perched high above the crowd, their perseverance in the name of 'free speech', ours in the name of tolerance.

A large police presence gathered. They mostly observed. Scuffles broke out. Midday turned to dusk. The police retired.

We took turns on the megaphone saying our piece. The NO campaigners stood there still, determined they would triumph like martyrs. Someone threw hummus at their sign. Knee-deep in blue chalk, my friend interrupted me as I scrawled, 'Secular means fuck off.' She handed me a tub of glitter. 'Oh yes,' I smirked.

Glitter filled the air. We danced among it like children in the eternal gardens. We threw it in all directions, on them and on ourselves. We doused their signs in it. We laughed and we mocked as the perseverance melted from their faces. We coloured the avenue with it like it was our war paint. The sunset dwindled and the campus began to empty. Both sides knew this minor battle had ended, both of the assumption they were the victors, but the war had only just begun.

I returned home the night of the protest, huge grin on my face from a successful day of pissing off homophobes. Until I saw it: the footage.

'The footage you are about to watch was captured on the 14th of September 2017, at the University of Sydney as pro same-sex marriage advocates surrounded and overran an information stand upholding traditional marriage.'

The entire event had been filmed. Albeit cleverly edited, placing me front and centre. There I was, stealing their signs, screaming, yelling, and throwing an assortment of products at them. Infamous commentator Andrew Bolt time-stamped some of the footage's finest moments:

> 58:58 'No' student assaulted.
> 1:51:30 'Yes' student grabs for sign, appears to kick.
> 1:52:00 Pushing and shoving, glitter thrown: 'I want to stomp on your heads, it would be beautiful!'
> 1:52:46 Woman pours red dye and glitter.
> 1:53:22 More glitter and dye thrown.
> 1:54:35 Sign destroyed, abuse, shouting down.

I could hear it in my voice, the anger, the hurt and the pain. I knew I had been moments away from crying, but the world did not. I had become trapped in their intricately woven web of conservatism and hate. The NO campaigners labelled themselves the martyrs of free speech.

Perhaps I was the martyr?

With my bedroom door locked, eyeballs glued to the cool blue of the screen, I tortured myself by reading any mention of the event. *The Herald Sun* labelled it 'Sydney University's Gay Marriage Thugs Attacking NO Students.' Some of the press was kinder, 'Police Called as Hundreds of Protesters Surround Sydney University's "Vote No" Rally.' But this event was the first chance to look unkindly on the otherwise love-driven YES campaign, and it spread like wildfire. With the domination of their narrative, I began to believe it, to feel it, and live it. As I stared back at the person on screen, someone I could no longer recognise, I saw myself as a setback to the movement – as a betrayer.

I spent days with a blanket wrapped around my entire body for safety. I couldn't eat but my stomach continued to empty itself of bile. Too scared to leave the house, I had to explain the situation to my lecturers, I did not feel safe to go to class, let alone be out in public.

Severe depression and anxiety are old friends of mine. I had struggled with these lingering pests from the age of thirteen. But these thoughts weren't welcome when it was no longer my own brain telling me I ought to die, but the general public. I had never experienced true fear for my safety – until I was instructed by the free legal service on campus to go incognito – change my number, stay hooded, delete any social media accounts, dye my hair to something less distinguishable. Disappearing seemed the easiest course of action, I just never anticipated that I would go under the radar for two whole years.

But there was no choice.

My details and usual whereabouts did the rounds on obscure fascist websites, even writing that I frequented the local bar. I stopped going. My mobile constantly rang. I would foolishly answer it. Those mostly one-sided calls instructed me to shove a glass jar so far up my ass, or, the blunter of the bunch told me they were just going to find me and kill me.

The calls, the voicemails, they still echo in my mind.

Walking to the bus stop one day, I listened to the voicemails and I felt hopeless, the weight of my actions too heavy to bear, alone in a war much larger than myself. As I waited for the bus to arrive, I received a message from a mutual friend. Nobody I knew too well; in fact, we had not officially met. 'I can see you at the bus stop from my apartment,' she wrote. I cranked my neck left, then right, but could not see her.

'Where?' I replied.

'Look for the flag.'

In the corner of my eye, I saw her waving the rainbow flag from her apartment window. It triumphed with the wind among all the hate that surrounded it. It brought a smile to my face. But as I looked closer, I could see commotion from the window. A man yelled, pulling the flag inside against her will. 'I am so sorry,' she wrote back. 'My landlord was inspecting and said he would kick me out for flying a rainbow flag.' She was fighting her own battle. We all were.

In the background, the larger war continued to rage on. We had set the tone. After us murals were destroyed, people were hurt, and slurs became the norm.

Most friends congratulated me. They would buy me a beer and introduce me as that kid that stole the sign, but I still felt like I had betrayed them.

Once all the postal ballots had been counted, a YES vote was declared – sixty percent in favour. That day was one of the happiest days of my life. I felt as if the cross they forced me to bear had vanished. I could stretch my arms. 'Maybe everything will be okay,' I thought. Celebratory champagnes turned into day-drinking.

We paraded the streets like we owned the place – we fucking did.

Because we fought for it.

It took many months before I realised that I had become genuinely traumatised by the event and its aftermath. Since the barrage of threats, I had tried to repress the memory of the protest and all things related to it. The postal survey became a sore topic of discussion for me. I refused to watch the footage of the protest, even to this day. Two years of forced severe introversion had me nostalgic for life before university. I despised high school, yearning to lurch free from the spiked perimeter fence and face the real world.

Yet, I faced it head-on, fast. As I learnt more about the world around me, I swore injustice would end someday. Naïve I was, only to learn a monstrosity defended the right to bigotry with every sharpened tooth and vicious claw.

I faced the beast head-on and it chewed me to pieces.

NIGHTCLUBBING

Harold Legaspi

Iggy Pop sang his little
heart out on my ghetto
blaster before I refused
to line up, flashing the bouncers
at Palms, or wait, was it Stonewall?
before doing the walk of shame to Arq.

When you've been doing it since the
days of DCMs, among the sadists,
spies and hippies, the Ithica street crew,
the COFA artistes, up on podiums,
topless, sweating, swearing
before the night
turns to a snore,
you become possessed with
ecstasy, poison-fuelled nostalgia
and enough inertia to
punch through walls with
a look.

GONE BOY

Harold Legaspi

The days
Such a disappointment

When you'd go trawling for more
Of that poison
That made our relationship
Toxic

We met only once
Told our dreams over
A cup of coffee
Because we could

Yet you never heard
The quiver in my voice
That said rescue me
From them

You threw me back in with
The dogs

Without thinking of the
Consequences

May as well have never met you
Instead I hold on to this
Memory of you and I together
The salt of me upon your lips
That reverberating sensation
Of thickened skin and blood
Gushing
To our manhood

I wrote you a rose
Shaped of paper and ink
Which you denied
Because for some reason
It was not meant to be
The paper entrails of the morning after
Severed from lust, possible romance
The way your eyes settled on mine
To carry your weight

Life's complexities
Simplified by your iron will to reject
To say no
Right after letting me in

I only scratched the surface
I felt acid burning my face
I am deformed
You don't realise just what you took away
The years of weathered chastity
Of patience, waiting for him
Him that wasn't you
It was never you
Forgetting to trust my own instincts, my dreams
As if they meant nothing
Cheap as the faux cologne you wore that night
Marks a little death of sorts
In passing

KYLIE

Adelia Croser

There have been many regrets in the decade since my mother passed. There are the regrets for the things I didn't do – telling her that I loved her enough, being there when she passed, or asking more questions about her life. Then there are the regrets for things she'll never be able to do – to be there for a graduation, a wedding, a birth – or that she'll never be able to fill in the blanks where 'I'll tell you when you're older' stands, or where my memory fails me.

My mother was always relatively open with me and my sister, she used to say that we were so easy to talk to. 'You've always got such a mature take on things; it really helps me to put things into perspective.' I'll never be sure if we ever helped her like she said, or if it's more like what my sister thinks, 'She always seemed to share things that happened to her when she was around the same age that we were. It was like she was sharing her child self with us in order to connect.' Perhaps it was neither. Perhaps it was both.

Whatever the reasons, it's led to some confusing questions that don't really have answers. I remember my mother going to a Cardiology Clinic when I was about twelve to get examined.

If pressed, I would say that it was because someone else in the family, my aunt, my grandmother, had recently been diagnosed with a genetic condition, and her family had all been recommended to get it checked out just in case. If my father was pressed, he would say he doesn't remember, 'But your mother was a bit of a hypochondriac, she probably just scared herself and got tested.'

It's hard to know the truth there. The truth is that my mother did have books on anxiety and panic attacks, and she always had certain things that scared her more than others. The truth is that she was terrified of leaded petrol. She would yell at my dad in the car if he had his window down when he drove into a petrol station. But that doesn't give me an answer. Was it an undiagnosed panic attack that she felt she needed to check out, or was it an advised routine test?

This wasn't the only thing my mother never told me the full story of, but it is the one I am constantly reminded of. 'Do you have any family medical history that we need to know about?' or 'Does your family have a history of heart conditions?' 'Maybe' isn't really enough at the doctor's office.

Kylie was another one of those things Mum told me. A story that I heard a little of, enough to try and create a mental image, but never enough to have any real idea of what happened.

***

'Have I ever told you about Kylie?' My mother asked me and my sister.

It wasn't one of those moments you remember the details of, not like 'I remember it as though it happened yesterday.' If you ask me, we were talking, gathered around the kitchen table. If you ask my sister, we were driving back from somewhere – the shops? Violin lessons?

She hadn't mentioned Kylie before.

'Well, when my family used to live in Sydney, we lived next door to another family, who had a daughter called Kylie. One day, we were in the backyard playing chasey with Kylie and she grabbed onto one of the poles lining our back porch. She was electrocuted and she died.'

I can remember not knowing what to say, and just staying silent. What do you say to that?

Mum didn't seem particularly upset by what she was saying, and I wasn't sure why she was telling us. Was she trying to warn us about electricity? About water? Could it really have happened? It seemed impossible.

'I wish I'd kept in better contact with the family,' she said. 'They were so lovely. It must have been heartbreaking for them.'

***

When I moved to Sydney, I brought the family photographs with me, to pass on to my sister for safekeeping. I would scan them and keep digital copies, while she kept the originals, so that between us, the photos would be safe. Just in case. With us now living in separate states for the first time in our lives, it seemed important. I was scanning the photos when I came across Kylie again, in a small photo of two children sitting on Santa's lap, on the back written 'Kylie & Bradley, Ryde'.

It's a small, yellow-toned photo. Kylie's on the left, sitting on Santa's knee, looking at someone off camera, smiling in that awkward way children do when asked to. Was it her mum saying, 'Smile Kylie, say cheese!' Or the photographer? Bradley sat on the other knee, caught open-mouthed and unaware. If it were any other photo, I wouldn't have kept it, but it's proof that my mother really did know a Kylie – that her story was real.

***

The next time I went to visit my sister, photographs in tow, I asked her if she remembered Mum telling us about Kylie.

'Of course.' My sister almost took it as an affront that she might not remember. That I'd accuse her of forgetting something about Mum. 'Why?'

She'd always held on tighter than me. Of the two of us, she's the one who holds onto the physical objects that made up our mother's daily existence. She has the small wooden cross that my mother held during chemo. The purse that always carried photographs of the two of us. She has the lipstick that she hardly wore, and the necklace that she always did.

'I was going through the photographs the other day. You

remember the one of the kids on Santa's lap? We could never figure out who they were. That was Kylie, and Bradley.'

'Oh! I guess that makes sense, they'd be about the right age. They were all pretty young at the time.'

As I looked over at her, she's looking down at the photograph with an expression on her face that I imagine I also had when I looked at it. The feeling that you've lost something you can't get back.

'What do you remember Mum saying about it? About Kylie?'

It's a familiar conversation – passing memories back and forth. Last Christmas morning, my sister, my mum's sister Diana, her girls and I all sat at the table after our annual breakfast and passed around stories of Mum. My parents' families grew up in the same small country town and so my aunt and dad have a long history of common experiences. Every family gathering eventually devolves into 'Do you remember that person who ... ' or 'How about that one time when ... ' and 'Oh, I heard from so-and-so the other day, turns out they're divorced now.' Mostly it's things I'm familiar with, but sometimes it's not. Thankfully, Christmas is mostly filled with joy now, rather than sadness.

My sister took a moment, looked down at the photograph and then put it to one side.

'She was the next-door neighbour's kid, right? She was the one who died in their backyard.'

'That's the one. Do you remember how it happened?'

'I think it was something to do with the lights in the backyard.

Maybe they weren't installed properly? I think they were fairy lights, you know, those string ones that go across the porch?'

I looked at her for a moment and wondered whether it was worth asking if she thought she could be wrong. That hadn't always gone so well in the past.

'I thought it was a spotlight.'

'Maybe? I just remember that the lights were touching the pole that Kylie grabbed.'

As we sat there, I said, 'I can't remember anything else. Just that. Just that it was a spotlight in their backyard. Do you remember anything else?'

'You know, I do have this one image in my head. That they tucked Kylie into bed after it happened. That the adults had picked her up off the ground and carried her to bed. Mum said that she had no idea what was happening, that she thought Kylie was just sleeping. Isn't that weird? That a child died, and they just put her to bed. I guess they were waiting for an ambulance or something.'

I don't remember that at all, and I'm grateful. It's a stark image I'm glad I haven't had in my head all these years. How did she cope with it? Is it worse now that she has a face to put to the body?

'I guess there was one other thing. Mum never really talked about how she felt about Kylie's death, but she did talk about how guilty her dad felt.'

I don't remember Mum telling us that either. Why did he feel guilty? What could he possibly have done?

'I think he installed the lights? He must have blamed himself.'

I'm suddenly thankful for my sister. We haven't always been nice to each other, but she's shared all my experiences with me, and I can always rely on her to help fill those gaps in my memory.

***

Kylie, and the photo, stuck with me for weeks after I got back to Sydney. As I spent my days travelling between my house, the CBD, and the university campus, I thought about Kylie. Did she walk past Town Hall and marvel at how big and beautiful it was? Did her parents, or my grandparents, take their families to Luna Park? Did they wander in between the rides eating fairy floss? Did they visit the Sydney Opera House and see a show there?

I wanted to find out more about Kylie. To walk around Ryde and go visit the house she lived in. To see if I can find any information.

***

The New South Wales State Library is this huge imposing building up past Hyde Park, backing onto the Botanical Gardens. I walked there one day, going past all the works happening around Martin Place as the new Sydney Metro system was being built. I haven't seen a Sydney that isn't covered in scaffolding and fencing. The Sydney I know has a cramped and dirty feel to it. People getting crushed into smaller and smaller spaces, while new construction sites cover the city in dust.

Walking into a foyer off to the side of the main building, I was struck by how modern it looked. It had a lovely open glass space with a wide circular staircase leading down to the lower floors. So far, I haven't found Sydney people particularly friendly, and the first two people I asked for help to find the microfilm archives are true to form: brusque, business-like and efficient. 'Down those stairs and talk to the librarian there,' and 'You can't take your backpack in but there's lockers back there, then go through here, down those steps and talk to another librarian.' It definitely feels like Sydney.

The next librarian, however, took the time to show me around. She seemed a little younger than me, and not entirely confident about how the microfilm archive worked, but together we figured it out.

I had googled around a little bit before visiting the library, trying to find a direction to start searching in. I only had an idea of the year that it had happened, between 1972 and 1973, that my aunt had provided in a short conversation. I had the names my aunt knew Kylie's parents by too, Reena and Blue Thurgar, but she didn't know their full names or how to spell them. The first result that came up was a private ancestry.com listing for Kylie Thurgar. Possibly correct, but not enough to go on. The next, an oddly trite website called Heaven's Address, listed cemetery plaques and gravestones within a small NSW area.

There, in small letters, the website read, 'Kylie Thurgar / passed away on 15 July 1973 / aged four years.' I'm so used to being able to google and find out someone's whole world from their social media. It felt strange that Kylie had been reduced to such a small caption, an image of a plaque and a pinpoint location on a map. But the date was something to go on, 15 July 1973.

I thought that there should be an article in an old newspaper. It's one of those attention-getting tragedies that the media relies on to sell newspapers, 'Four-Year-Old Dies in Freak Backyard Accident,' or 'Careless Electrician Kills Four-Year-Old'.

The newspapers with the largest circulation are in drawers that line one side of the library. So much history condensed into such a small space. Two weeks of newspapers in a tiny box.

The Sydney Morning Herald is the daily newspaper for the Sydney area, founded in 1831 as the *Sydney Herald.* It's sold nationwide. Surely, I could find something there.

There were a few other people using the microfilm machines. There was an older man who sat to the left of me. He wasn't like the usual well-dressed businessmen I'm used to seeing around the CBD, he looked more like he was from the other side of Sydney – the people struggling to pay their rent, or homeless on the streets. I wondered what he was doing. Was he researching his own family history? The woman who sat on the other side of me was well dressed and looked out of place, asked me to show her how to use the microfilm equipment.

I started with a copy of *The Sydney Morning Herald* dated

16 July 1973, thinking there would be something around then. There's nothing. Nothing on the 16th. Nothing on the 17th. It wasn't until the 18th that I noticed the death notices section and realised I might've missed something. Going back to the 17th, I saw it.

> THURGAR. Kylie. – 15 July 1973, at hospital, late of Putney, dearly loved daughter of Mr and Mrs Vincent Thurgar and loving sister of Bradley, aged four years.
> In God's care.
> See Wednesday's 'Herald' for funeral details.
> – *The Sydney Morning Herald* – 17 July 1973

Scrolling through to Wednesday 18, I found the funeral notice.

> THURGAR. – Relatives and friends of Mr and Mrs Vincent Thurgar, of Putney, are invited to attend the funeral of their daughter, KYLIE, to leave St Chad's Church, corner of Delange Road and Morrison Road, Putney, tomorrow (Thursday) after a service commencing at 10 a.m. for the Northern Suburbs Crematorium.
> – *The Sydney Morning Herald* – 18 July 1973

This was it. This was all *The Sydney Morning Herald* had to say. A young child was ripped away from her family and this was all there was about it. It barely said anything.

'15 July 1973, at hospital.' I always thought she died instantly.

My sister thought she did too. But she didn't. Kylie held on right up until the hospital. Was she conscious at all? Did they get a chance to say anything to her? Did they still hope she'd be ok?

St Chad's Church is an Anglican church in Putney. It's not much to look at. My mother's family was also Anglican. Did the two families go to church together on Sundays, all dressed up in their Sunday best? Five girls, one boy, and four parents, all quietly sitting together, listening to a sermon. Regular church attendance was more common back then. The thought reminds me of attending church with my parents as a child, impatiently waiting for it to be over.

The Sydney Morning Herald doesn't say anything else on Kylie. Neither does *The Daily Telegraph*, which also ran during that time. If the bigger newspapers didn't have anything, maybe the local ones did?

The two local papers at the time were the *Northern District Times* and the *Weekly Times*, both focusing on the suburbs local to Ryde and Putney. They've got to be specially requested from where they're kept, on a little slip of paper that gets returned to you with the item, strangely archaic in a library that is using increasingly modern systems.

I looked through one, then the other. Nothing. Not a single thing about Kylie. The headlines from the week she died read, 'Special Warning Signs Not Needed' and 'Hunter's Hill Mayor Attacks Labor Policy'. Was it because the family wanted it to be kept quiet? Did the newspaper only cover things that were considered 'necessary' for everyone to know? Were the newspapers trying to be sensitive so that the Thurgars could grieve in peace, without neighbours dropping in with their overbearing condolences?

It may have been a kindness then, but it doesn't help me to figure out what happened now.

***

Ryde's main library is part of the recently refurbished Top Ryde City Shopping Centre, a beautiful modern building, originally built in 1957. It's full of wide glass windows, and cleanly sloping white plastic.

I had an appointment with the local history librarian, who has a small office in the back and keeps all the 'important' books under lock and key in a glass cabinet next to her desk.

As I talked to her she said, 'You know, it'd be easier if you wanted information about what Ryde was like back in the 1880s. We've got way more about that period. More recent history is surprisingly difficult.'

She's not wrong, the local history books are ninety-eight per cent historical Ryde, and only two percent more recent. She sent me towards a few books, census records, some photographs. It's not much. There's no real answers to be found here.

As I looked at electoral rolls for the years surrounding Kylie's death, I found both families on the records, 'V. Thurgar. 10 Charles Street, Putney,' and 'B. Blacklock. 5 Hordern Avenue, Putney.'

My aunt had only been able to remember that her family's house was near a small park with a memorial to Bennelong, an elder of the Eora people. Bennelong, it turns out, is buried at 25 Watson Street in an unmarked grave, in a location my mother would have walked past every day. It's strange to think that something so significant to so many people could go unnoticed for so long.

The census data and books on the other hand make it clear that Ryde was a very different place in the 1970s. Back then the northern part of Ryde still had orchards that were slowly being replaced by development and the Civic Centre had only just been built in 1963, later extended in 1972 to include a function space. The majority of the population was Anglo-Saxon and Anglican. Like my family. As I looked around the library space, it may have only given me a small snapshot, but it's very clear that Ryde is increasingly multicultural, and Anglicans are now only a minority.

Things have definitely changed since the 1970s.

***

As I flipped through some photos of past Ryde and Putney, my aunt called. I hadn't spoken to her properly in a while, although we'd been talking a little about Kylie.

She was the youngest of the four girls, and was around Kylie's age when the incident happened, so her memories are faint. She has, however, spent years with it, an unspoken elephant in her family's history.

I asked her if there was anything she did remember, like how soon afterwards they moved from Ryde to Adelaide.

'I remember we were living in the Normanville Pub by January 1974? We spent New Years' there. So uh, how long was that?'

'Kylie passed away in July 1973, so six months earlier,' I told her. 'Your family moved to South Australia within six months of Kylie's death.' She hmmed a little in assent. 'Lauren said that she remembered Mum talking about how guilty Grandad felt about Kylie. How much he carried her death with him. She thought it must have been Grandad who installed the light. Do you remember that?'

'We never really talked about it, so I really don't know, maybe? I think it might've been an electrician who installed the lights though.'

'You moved so soon though; Grandad must've started planning to move quickly afterwards. And to bring a family up in a hotel. Did you ever consider that the guilt as well as the easy access to alcohol contributed to his addiction?' She was silent for a moment. I continued, 'Was he an alcoholic before it happened?'

'I think he was already using it as a coping mechanism before it happened. But perhaps it wasn't as bad before.'

It was never something I'd considered. My grandfather's alcoholism and the effect it had on my family was a fact I'd grown up with. I knew him simply as an alcoholic who'd died shortly after I was born. He'd never been real enough to me to consider why he was an alcoholic, or what he was dealing with that made him turn to alcohol in the first place. Was this it?

Was this what triggered so many of my mother's family issues? Was this why my grandma was always taking in strays and showed them more love and affection than her own children? It's probably not something I'll ever really know, but I saw my grandfather in a new light, as someone who had struggled and felt deeply.

It also made it a little easier to understand how my mother could have forgiven him for his alcoholism. She'd once told me and my sister about an incident where he'd been driving drunk off his face, her older sister in the front seat, and the three younger girls in the back seat, terrified and screaming. I'd never understood how she reconciled that memory with the father she loved. Perhaps this was it, with a little bit of understanding of why he might've been that way.

My aunt continued, 'There's something else actually. I don't remember much else but, I once heard my mother say, "Why did it take their only daughter, when I have four?"'

How do you cope as a child hearing that? To my mum and aunts, it must've sounded like 'It should have been you'. My sister and I have always been open with each other about the fact that we would've preferred losing our dad to cancer, rather than our mum. But it's always been between us, and we'd never dream of telling him that, whether he suspects it or not.

'Did you keep in contact with the Thurgars much after you moved?'

'They visited us once in South Australia a few years later, but after that my mother discouraged me from contacting them, saying "Don't bother them, they don't need the reminder." That didn't stop me though, I visited them a few times over the years, when we moved back to the East Coast, a few times since then.'

'Did you ever talk to them about Kylie? During one of the times you saw them?'

My aunt has visited once or twice in the last decade, and she plans on visiting them again soon. But when I ask her about what it's like visiting with them, she confesses that even she feels guilty about it. She's afraid that they'll think that she's only keeping in contact with them for their money as they'll likely outlive their remaining child, Bradley, who has Down Syndrome. She's also worried that her presence is a painful reminder of Kylie, one that they don't want.

'A few years back, Reena and I went and visited the plaque in the cemetery where she was cremated. It was the first time she'd been there in thirty years. The last time she'd visited with Bradley he'd run off and they spent half an hour looking for him. She couldn't bring herself to return since then. We also visited the old house, on Hordern Avenue, and asked the current owners if we could go into the backyard. She just sat there, quietly crying. I don't think she's ever really made peace with it.'

After we hung up, she emailed over a few more photos that she had. Both of the photos look like happy, normal families. You wouldn't ever be able to guess that there was a tragedy hiding in these photos. You wouldn't guess that one family was missing their only daughter, and that the other hid intense guilt and a burgeoning alcoholic.

***

Modern-day Putney is a very affluent suburb, being as close to the city as it is, with beautiful older houses that still have the same facades that they did when they were built. There's also the modern-style houses that have clearly been built in the last few decades. It's a response to the huge influx of money into the area.

Hordern Avenue felt pretty emblematic of the suburb as a whole. As I walked up the street there's a strange divide between the left side of the street, all big open modern houses, and the right side, that looked like they're the original houses built on the blocks. Number Five is at the top of the cul-de-sac, and right now, it's hidden behind trees. If it was any other house, I might have thought it was cosy, but knowing what I know, it felt sinister and shadowy, hiding the trauma of its previous occupants behind its leaves.

Number Five Hordern Avenue has had a bit of a makeover since 1973, but it's still recognisable. It's the same set of windows in the front left of the house that are in the old photo. The brickwork at the bottom had been replaced by similar wood panelling to make it uniform, and there was a big bush that was planted in front of the window. It looked so different from the light and airy feel of the house in 1973.

The house on the right had a few kids playing out the front on their tricycles with their dad quietly watching them, the perfect image of happy suburbia. Was my mother's family like this in 1973? Happily playing outside with their parents fondly watching over them?

I waved, and he waved back, but I wished for a moment that they weren't there, so I could be there without feeling like someone was watching me, judging me for being there.

***

After I left Hordern Avenue, I walked over to Charles Street, where the Thurgars live. It's the same house they lived in then – it turns out it wasn't just next door, but a few streets over. Even this small detail I'd remembered wrongly. I can't imagine it, living in the same house all this time. My mother's family moved interstate within six months, while they've stayed here with the shadows of those memories all this time.

I wanted to go in and talk to them about Kylie. I wanted them to fill the holes in my memory, the holes in the stories from my mother and my aunt. But I couldn't. I couldn't ask them to relive that for me.

The story of Kylie is one with holes that can't be filled in. And I have to live with that.

THE FIRST SATURDAY IN MARCH

John Hannaford

The night air is still. According to our calendars, the arrival of autumn was a few days back, but the sticky Sydney humidity is still oppressive. Summer seems to last longer and longer.

Tonight, the streets of Darlinghurst are packed with people. The street is illuminated, brighter than usual. Mixing with the incandescence of the streetlights are coloured lights, temporarily strung up. Every colour of the spectrum is shining bright, fighting against the darkening sky. The shimmer of black asphalt is enhanced by the brilliant assortment of lighting and reflects a kaleidoscope of colour.

The atmosphere is electric. I can feel it. I know they are coming; I can feel their presence before I can hear them. The vibration of the air seems apparent even before the soundwaves arrive. Then the noise comes. Simultaneously I hear a low rumble and a shrill pitch, and it unleashes something primal.

With the combined roar of massed motorbikes and the shriek of their horns – almost like birdsong – the Dykes on Bikes herald the arrival of Sydney's Gay and Lesbian Mardi Gras parade.

Hundreds of bikes perform their procession along the parade

route. Their bikes are donned with gay apparel: pride flags flutter from handlebars and coloured gels taped to the headlamps create waves of illumination that match the stripes of the pride flag. Every bike features both a rider and a pillion passenger. Acres of flesh are on display. Leathers, both motorcycle and fetish. It is a celebration of life, on two wheels.

The Dykes on Bikes have had the honour of leading the parade since 1991. The position of the riders at the front of the parade is for an entirely practical reason: the bikes need to move at their own pace, unconstrained by the walkers and vehicles. An overheated bike stalling on the parade route would lead to a domino effect that would delay proceedings for the remainder of the night.

The history of the Dykes on Bikes is remarkable. A group of women riders from Sydney visited San Francisco in the late 1980s and were inspired by the original chapter of Dykes on Bikes that led proceedings at San Francisco Pride. Inspired by this radical reinvention of hyper-masculine biker culture, Sydney's Dykes on Bikes began patrolling the darkened streets of Darlinghurst and Kings Cross, keeping an eye on the gay, lesbian and transgender community.

This community, that sought the protections and comforts that came from frequenting gay pubs and clubs, found themselves at risk outside of them. From those early days patrolling the streets, grew a movement that came to support all members of the community.

It was a riot, then and now

The first Mardi Gras was held in June 1978 in solidarity with the international movement for gay rights on the anniversary of the 1969 Stonewall riots. The organisers wanted Mardi Gras to be equal parts a celebration and a protest. While the first Mardi Gras was met with police brutality, it became a movement that continued to mix celebration with protest. The subsequent Mardi Gras parades created a tradition that has grown exponentially.

There is something truly remarkable about the Mardi Gras parade. To close down part of a city and devote its busiest streets to a celebration of diversity is a remarkable feat. To do so every year, for more than forty years, is extraordinary. And to do so while remaining relevant and fresh is a testament to the continued value of Mardi Gras.

A logistical exercise like no other

The planning that goes into parade night is tremendous. There are few events of this scale in Australia. There are even fewer pride parades that happen at night, under lights, with marchers and vehicles. The planning for the evening exceeds twelve months, beginning even before the preceding parade has finished its procession up Oxford Street. I know because, for many years now, I've been one of those people that makes the night happen. Mardi Gras is an organisation that survives because of the dedication of an army of volunteers who work alongside talented staff, artists and producers. A rich tapestry of history is woven from the stories of those, like me, who dedicate their time to make Mardi Gras the success it is each year.

My story with Mardi Gras began in 2007 when I attended my first parade. It was an experience like no other. For the first time in my life I found a vibrant and loving community of people like me. And once a year the roads of Sydney were closed for this remarkable celebration of diversity and pride. While I adored the sights and sounds of Mardi Gras, I came to realise that the experience of those watching was not a patch on the experience of those in matching t-shirts over the other side of the barricades. I knew I needed to return the following year as a volunteer.

I joined the Sydney Gay and Lesbian Mardi Gras family in 2008. I was one of those thousands of volunteers that collectively worked to make the parade happen. That year, the thirtieth anniversary of the parade, was the year that I found my chosen family. I found in me a voice, a passion, a set of skills and an experience that was lacking in my life. I grew a little that year and have grown every year since. The roles I have performed and the hours that I dedicated have gradually increased as time has passed.

There are so many stories that are created each year at the parade. More than 300,000 people pack the streets of Sydney, while a group of 12,500 follow the Dykes on Bikes up that sacred tarmac of Oxford Street. A team of more than 1,600 volunteers marshal together to make the parade the success it is. With a history now entering its fifth decade, those Mardi Gras stories intermingle from year to year and person to person and grow and morph into legends. Some of those stories pass from legend to infamy and live on. From the darkest days of illness and loss in the 1980s to the explosion of joy that followed the 2017 marriage equality postal survey, Mardi Gras has been the place where my community celebrates their shared identity and tells their story.

Volunteers are the heart of Mardi Gras

I've never marched the parade route. I see that hallowed ground as being the territory of my community. That tarmac is a stage upon which my community is given the spotlight to express themselves for one night. I don't seek that spotlight, but I work damn hard to ensure that the spotlight is shone upon our parade entrants. For me, the role I perform as a volunteer is alongside those entrants. One cannot exist without the other.

Many years ago, at a briefing for volunteers ahead of the start of Mardi Gras, an elder of the organisation spoke to our group and told us of a conversation they had with their mother earlier that day. In describing their plan to soon meet and speak with volunteers, this person's mother offered a valuable insight:

> To volunteer is to give the most precious gift of all. Your time. Time is a precious commodity that cannot be recouped or recalled or clawed back. The devotion of your time to a cause is sacred. The devotion of this time with a common

purpose alongside others – as a volunteer – morphs from the sacred to the divine.

That moment – that recounted conversation – proved to be a revelation for me. I entered that room expecting to learn some unremarkable instructions. When I left the briefing that day, I knew that my path forward would include greater commitment to volunteering. That year was the last year that I worked as a general volunteer and I began my ongoing commitment to the organisation.

In the years that have followed I have led various teams at a range of Mardi Gras events, worked alongside NSW Police in the parade command centre, rapidly developed my (limited) driving skills on a golf buggy within the safe confines of the parade route and even voiced the announcements at Mardi Gras Party. In 2017 I joined the Mardi Gras Board where I have been proud to help lead the organisation.

Here we are once again

The remarkable thing about attending Mardi Gras is that very few people find themselves attending by happenstance or accident. Meticulous planning, fastidious costuming, exquisite makeup and copious accessorising are all common tenets of us Mardi Gras revellers. Admittedly, given the size of the event, the planning that goes into the night easily goes awry and the makeup and costuming has a tendency to quickly be discarded. But, for a moment, all of us present have brought our whole selves. We are here to celebrate our differences and rejoice in our common links. We come together for one night, in one place, to celebrate humanity, life and love.

In that moment that the Dykes on Bikes herald the arrival of yet another Mardi Gras parade, I feel connected. I feel connected to the history of those that came before me, those that raged into the night in a flurry of sequins and satin and fought for liberty and visibility. I feel connected to the people we lost to the HIV/AIDS crisis of the 1980s and in the years since. I feel connected to those entrants who devoted themselves to developing choreography: always in a forwards direction, never backwards. I feel connected to the many volunteers and committee members that toiled together to build an organisation that can bring this multifaceted community together for one night of the year.

The connection that I feel to the past is echoed by the connection I feel to those who will follow in my footsteps. My time with Mardi Gras represents only a small portion of its history and my influence has been modest, but when I look back over the years during which I gave my time, I am proud. I am proud to have added my threads to the tapestry of Mardi Gras history. And I know that there will be many more that will follow and add their threads once I have stepped away.

I keenly feel the approach of the Dykes on Bikes at parade each year because, in that moment, I think back to how I felt that first time I attended. Somewhere in the crowd is a person who will come to realise that they – no matter where they are on their journey in life – are not alone. They will find their tribe. This is why I celebrate pride. This is why I volunteer with the Sydney Gay and Lesbian Mardi Gras.

THE SHAME OF PRIVILEGE

James Mukheibir

A life marked by the shadow of white guilt.[1]

These words seem to pulsate on the page in front of me. Pulsate with rage. Pulsate with pain. There is an uncomfortable weight in my belly. I feel a little unwell. The words, staggered across the paper, get under my skin and keep going, squirrelling their way into the dark recesses of my heart and mind. These hidden places where my embarrassment hides, shy away from the light of self-reflection. My embarrassment at my identity and what it represents to so many.

I am South African. And I am white.

It is a part of me that remains a source of conflict. In most areas of my life, I see myself as my own person. I don't often consider those who came before me, preferring to define myself by my own actions and experiences. But the reality of where I was born clings to my conscience and refuses to let go. People like me built a country around the idea that they were better

1 This personal essay was written in response to Nayyirah Waheed's poem 'White Guilt' found on page 214 of *Salt*, a collection of Waheed's poetry.

than the black and coloured kids that I went to school with. They built a country designed to give me every opportunity to succeed; for me to reach great heights, propped up on the backs of those oppressed. My privilege was made possible by stripping the humanity from generations of African hearts.

I never saw apartheid in its legislative form. I never experienced it as an enforced policy. It was always referred to in the same tone as the Dark Ages were, by parents and teachers and in news reports. A time of massacres and dystopic political control, a time ended by the bravery and humanity of freedom fighters. There was an atmosphere of rebirth in South Africa throughout my childhood. South Africa could now stand united and strong. Yet through a child's innocent eyes, the deep scars left by generations of racial oppression were glaringly obvious. My country felt like a train carriage full of people trying desperately not to stare at the glossy disfigurements of a burn victim, simultaneously hypnotised by their wounds and doing everything in their power to avoid acknowledging their existence. In no way did this remove the existence of the problem.

Pressures in the white community to remain positive about the new South Africa allowed many to pretend that the damage was relegated to the past, along with the regime itself. Young and oblivious to these pressures, I entered primary school and instantly noticed that things were different. Looking back, I am surprised by the detailed observations that I still remember, perhaps the consequence of a curious child confronted by things he didn't understand. When my third-grade teacher announced that we would be doing swimming for PE that term, I couldn't be more excited.

I had been going to swimming lessons since I was five years old and had a swimming pool in my backyard. Sitting on the side of the pool, watching others attempt to swim laps, I was given my first reality check; most of the black kids in my class had not been given the same opportunities as me. I didn't understand it at the time. Why hadn't their parents sent them to Tanya down the road to learn how to do backstroke? For the first time, I began to understand that I was privileged.

If I had been swimming with my classmates fifteen years earlier, half of them would not have been allowed in the same pool as I was and most likely wouldn't have been my classmates at all. The massacres may have been a thing of the past, but I walked into my school every day many steps ahead of my black peers. I had new school shoes, I watched educational TV shows and my parents were highly educated and helped me with my homework. I had a maid who made me lunch and a gardener who looked after my expansive backyard. Both black. Regardless of the arguments for job creation, there was an established hierarchy whereby grown adults had to serve me, an eight-year-old because I was born to have an easier path through life. Not because I worked harder or was more deserving, but because of what my predecessors had done, because I am white.

With this history acting as the kettle to the steam of my

achievements, how can I go on without seeing a stain discolouring my identity? How can I feel proud of who I am and what I have achieved? My privilege breeds discontent in what I have and what I see. All of my life, I have not been able to escape its cloying, sour taste. As I grew up, I realised I have accepted it, I have begun to see it as a reality of life. Content in my discontentedness.

Because that is what guilt is. It is the least productive of any human emotion. I feel guilty for my privilege and that benefits no one. It does not reduce the harm those of my race have inflicted on others. It does not lift up those who were born with darker skin. It is an act of recognition and nothing more. There is nothing progressive in this guilt – it simply sits and festers in my mind, uncomfortably twisting my stomach when I am confronted by inequalities and others abusing their privilege. It is a feeling that can easily leave me paralysed, aware of my advantage and impunity, but at a loss as to what to do about it.

I hesitate to come out as a crusader for racial equality, as the idea that I have any knowledge of the pain or struggles or even the best way forward for any person of colour feels like a perpetuation of my privilege. The expression of my feelings of guilt seems like a distraction from the issue at hand. Positioning myself as the victim of an uncomfortable reality inevitably engages a comparison of pain with those who are truly suffering at the hands of an inherently prejudiced society.

It once again centres the focus on the feelings of a white person in a dialogue that should have nothing to do with pandering to people like me. If we become a non-racial society like so many white allies claim they want to achieve, will it serve as absolution for the past actions of the white community? Are the efforts of well-meaning white people to undo the structural bias merely an act of penance? If so, is it really the best I can do?

Fighting for equality as a result of my white guilt feels like a service to my pride rather than any disadvantaged community. What does that leave as an alternative? Resting easy on the immense freedom afforded to me because of the colour of my skin? The white community is making no effort to offer a hand up to the people it has held down for so long. I have yet again found myself in the shadow of an excuse for inaction. While the argument for cultural autonomy is a valid one, it is not a means to wash our hands of responsibility and ignore the work required to achieve an equal society.

My drive to understand this deep-set discomfort in my relationship with the world is very much rooted in my own family history. My mum has told me stories since I was very young of my grandparents' efforts during apartheid. Their work has always inspired me to question my own actions. After starting and working with the Young Christian Workers (YCW) in South Africa, my grandfather and grandmother got involved in the beginnings of the black trade union movement in South Africa. The YCW was an organisation that believed in the fundamental equality of all people, and Eric and Jean Tyacke contributed to improving conditions for black African workers throughout the country. This involved travelling to townships such as Soweto, where white people were not known to go, working within those communities to educate workers about their rights and providing support in the early battles against employers for basic work and human rights. This work was illegal and both of them were banned from doing it by the government. This meant that they had to leave their work immediately by order of the Security Police; they weren't allowed to be involved in the publication of any material, were not allowed in any educational institution and were not allowed to be in the company of any other banned person.

Being a married couple, however, the government had to make a rare concession to allow them to be in each others' company. As the power of the regime was weakened over time by sanctions and dwindling public support, black trade unions were legalised, and my grandfather returned to work with the YCW for the rest of his career.

My mother's childhood was shaped by their attitudes, and my childhood was littered with stories about them and how her school friends were shocked walking into their house and seeing whites and blacks sitting together, drinking tea and chatting. 'What was unusual about my parents, particularly my father,' she says, 'is that he really had black friends. He always had a black social group, which was unusual even for those working against apartheid.' It was something that was completely opposite to the propaganda of the government at the time, but my grandparents didn't care. They did not let themselves become indoctrinated. They engaged with everyone as an equal. My late grandfather was a man unfazed by the questions that I am battling with. He saw people being treated badly and he found a way to contribute to the fight for a better world.

My family has nurtured me and my sister with these values as we grew into adults. Whether it was stories or actions, the value of empathy and service was an enduring theme. After I graduated from high school, I decided to take a year off to live in Cambodia, before going on to university. As a newly recognised adult and free from the structure of school, I was enamoured with the idea of going somewhere a little wild and passing on the knowledge that I had gained by teaching English in a small village. I was aware of how lucky I was to have received the private school education that I had, and I was eager to share it with those less advantaged than me. I arrived in Cambodia with optimism and a simple goal: to try and help those who needed it.

A first, everything seemed great. My classes were engaging and enriching, and my students had a desire to learn that I had never seen in an Australian school. I felt like I was genuinely making a difference to people's lives, and my own life was so much better for it. But there were also inherent issues that I had to confront. The international volunteers, myself included, lived in a compound above the school, separate from the village. It was a situation that garnered a white saviour complex in the volunteers. Sure, we were there to help the community but, removing ourselves from it created an inescapable superiority. As if the gates were unlocked for students to come and benefit from the generous souls who had come all this way to bestow knowledge on the peasants.

I, and one of the other Australian volunteers, fought hard to be allowed to live in the village and successfully organised a simple room above the house of a family. It was when I was actually living in the village, using their language to the best of my ability, cooking their food and living their lifestyle, that I realised that the majority of our interactions with the local community were based on the ideology of white supremacy.

The Westernisation of the world has reduced the value of their culture in our eyes. The idea that learning a language from an eighteen-year-old with no formal teaching training could enhance your chances of being 'successful' sounds absurd in theory but is the driving force behind volunteer projects such as the one I was involved in. Fluency in English has become an undeserving and inaccurate, but nonetheless prevalent, measure of intelligence and potential. Because of language, this emphasis inevitably elevates the perceived intellect of white people and led to my whiteness turning me into some form of celebrity in the village when I first arrived. People wanted to take photos with me. I was asked to go to the front of the queue when buying groceries and eyes would follow me through the streets as I made my way to class.

I was again faced with the reality that I was part of a system that perpetuated white dominance and privilege, one that positioned the advantages and successes that I have benefited from as something to aspire to. Even in the world of charity, white and Western supremacy is the foundation of the artificial hierarchy of power.

Throughout my life, I have seen the far-reaching, entrenched effects of the white power dynamics that have shaped much of history. So much of the comfort I have enjoyed has been a result of the advantages afforded to me for the skin I was born with. The burning shame that washed over me when I first read Nayyirah Waheed's words is not something I should work to dispel. This is not a burden that should weigh me down, but instead motivate me to never stop questioning the world and my attitudes towards it.

I came back from Cambodia and enrolled in the University of Sydney, and there I found an entire microcosm of culture and politics. I met passionate advocates and activists for the equality and rights of Aboriginal Australians and their perspective was always one of action. In a conversation I had with Akala Newman, a proud Aboriginal Australian student at the university and my friend, she expressed the need for the community to come together as one to support each other in this fight.

'It needs to be a collective effort with respect given to the voices of the people who it actually effects,' she says. 'It is important to know when to be quiet, you listen and you learn, and then you can go and talk to those who don't understand because as a white person, you have a voice and people will listen. We need to stop crying because it is still happening. We need to stand shoulder to shoulder and fight to get justice.'

Ultimately, I am a white man and I have freedom that some can only dream of. I will be listened to and, like my grandfather, I can use my freedom to empower those who do not have my privilege. I cannot speak for those who have suffered or decide what is best for them, but I have immense privilege and the power to change the world around me. I will probably never have definitive answers to my questions and discomfort.

Societies from around the world have come a long way but there is still so far to go. In order to keep moving towards our ideals of equality, we must recognise our own prejudices and privileges. I will never stop learning if I never stop questioning. With each new thing I learn, I can help challenge and educate those perpetuating the biases. There will always be a divide and I will never be able to change the world on my own.

But together we can face up to the uncertainties and discomforts and create a more cohesive and uplifting community. Perhaps, one day this generation and future generations of Cambodians, Africans, Aboriginal Australians and other marginalised people can employ their own agency and freedom to reshape and rebuild their world.

A world of their own imagination, not that of a white man's.

EMBODIMENT

Anastasia Taig

I birthed myself, Athena, from the father
Motherless and sexless
A woman in name only

Wired to the patriarchal mind,
I scorned the feminine mystique
The idol of the womb

My vessel was irrational, inadequate,
An obstacle that stood between
Me and self-realisation;

I raised my sword, ready to sever all
The parts that were made female and made wanting
Unsex myself and finally taste my freedom

But as the blade cut deep, I understood
That I had built my temple on their lies

Furnished my prison with their gods
Shamed my sisters and failed myself;

I cannot learn to be a woman
By listening to old men.

WHEN A KISS IS A QUEER, UNCERTAIN THING

Amy Wang

She paints the bedroom walls pink
like a prescription.
I kiss my reflection & tell her she's pretty
not because I am trying to like myself
not because I need someone to hold me
but just to see how it feels to kiss a girl.
These are the unpaid un-
imprisoned years,
where the start of maybe me &
end of maybe mine
is a faded watercolour/rippled mirror/
drunken laugh.
We spill questions like apologies onto the carpet
& look for answers in each other's bent bodies,
plant our fingers into each other's skin
like they will somehow,   in this barrenness,
grow into a useful thing. No

shame exists here
but the sorrysorrysorry shame (the mother tongue)
stuck on replay.
& I kiss my reflection
(who knew a kiss could feel this good)
just to make sure.

STRANGER IN DELHI

Grace Jing Johnson

Apsara

I was sitting with my father in the café on the fourth floor when I began to reminisce. We have come to this café since I was a child, where we have always waited for my mother to finish her shopping. It was still summer, and the shopping centre was busy with families and groups of schoolkids on holiday. My mother and I had just gotten back from a trip to India.

The waitress came to us through the crowded wooden tables and stood at our booth. She knew us well. Her hair, strands of dyed honey and emerging grey, was tied in a bun with loose strands. The new uniform had grey aprons and black t-shirts. She wore brown lipstick and smiled at us.

I ordered an iced coffee and a slice of carrot cake. My father had his usual flat white and Diet Coke.

'Thank you, Beth,' he said.

My father looked at the notepad slanted under his arm on the table. He was working on an article. He was always working to a deadline. Beth set the order on the table. I watched my father drink half the flat white in one steady swallow, never moving his eyes from the notepad, which had scrawls of pencil markings and arrows and crossing outs. He mumbled something to himself and then spoke to me, still half absent.

‘It is good you have some place to write about. A place you haven’t been to before.’

I nodded. But it was hard to write about a place you didn’t feel was yours, in any part of experiencing it. You needed to feel some part of it belonged to you first, or that you belonged to it. But what had happened in India was not so clear. That made it hard to write about too. But something he had always taught me to do was to write in my head, about what was happening around me and about what’s in my mind. If you can write about both, he had said, or about one but while implying the other, then you are learning something, and that is one of the most valuable things I can teach you.

So as we sat there in the shopping centre café, with people walking past in packs, and the glasses empty on the table now, and only crumbs and smeared icing left on the plate, and no notepad or pen for me to write with, I began to put it down, in my mind, as I remembered it.

My mother knew the family in India from her friends at work. She had made many Nepali friends at the nursing home and went to parties at their houses. Her closest friend’s family lived in New Delhi and told her they would look after her whenever she wanted to visit India. My mother said I should come before university started up again. I just had to pay for my plane ticket.

We stayed for one night at our stopover in Bangkok. It was hot but already I felt different being in a new place. The air was heavy and expectant, and everyone not walking seemed to be waiting for something. The Western men were sweating and their skin was red from the heat. Thai girls stood in front of the clothing stores and the bars with neon signs and blue lights. I remember thinking about the girls walking past, how beautiful they were, with young skin and black lined eyes, and how small their bodies were compared to mine. We moved with the crowd. I watched the workers in food stalls slicing fruit and stirring rice. In the Chinatown district, we had a dinner of flame-cooked prawns the size of my hand, and coconut water.

My mother's closest friend, Nisha, had arranged for her son to pick us up from the airport in New Delhi. Rahul is a very nice -looking boy, my mother told me in the customs line – she had met him once before in Nepal. But when I saw him waiting at the gate with flowers, and the way he said, 'Hi Aunty,' and how he seemed to shrink when I looked at him and said hello, I felt myself recoil. Also, he pronounced my name like 'Grease' and didn't look at me. But my mother liked him a lot. She joked that he was the son she always wanted. He was meek and pleasing, and went along with everything she said, and always said, 'Yes Aunty.' I followed them to the car, pushing a suitcase in each hand.

I'll always remember the taxi back to the hotel and seeing the streets of India for the first time – men urinating on the walls of the highway, cows walking between buses, children playing with rubble, faces peering out of helmets on the backs of dirty motorcycles. Stray dogs fought on the street and people sat under tents made of sheets and sticks. They seemed to live there. The streets were noisy and aggressive, and bikes cut in front of cars and taxi drivers yelled at bus drivers. I tried not to meet the eyes of the children crammed into rickshaws. The polite busboys dressed in red suits were taking our luggage into the lobby of a five-star hotel, the Leela Ambience Hotel.

The next day we took a taxi ten minutes away to meet the rest of Rahul's family, the Gurung family. They lived a right turn off the Gurgaon expressway in a complex of grey apartment buildings with dirt streets. People rode on motorcycles and pushbikes passed us with people with bags of groceries in one hand. There were dogs on the side of the brown gravel paths, all with the same brown fur matted by dirt. Their rib cages jutted, and their heads drooped.

'Is this place?' the driver asked.

'I don't know,' said my mother. Then a motorcycle came up beside the car. It was Rahul. He waved and he drove ahead of the car.

'Follow him,' she told the driver. And then to me, 'He is a very nice boy, isn't he?'

Nisha's sister, Gyani, was waiting at the door with her husband Kumar.

'My parents,' Rahul said to us.

'Namaste,' they said, and bowed. We did the same.

Gyani had a very round, plump face, and wore a bindi. Her hair was tied back, and she wore golden bangles on both wrists. She was dressed in orange and seemed to be always smiling and unaware. The father wore a simple brown fleece jumper with beige trousers and woven leather sandals. He had a kind but serious and tired face, and I saw my own father in his manner. They were very pleased to see my mother.

I looked at the walls as my mother gave them gifts of Australian chocolates and lotions. They spoke well together, all in varying degrees of broken English. They patted me on the back and smiled at me. The blue walls had on them carefully painted yellow flowers and the white walls were covered in a red leaf pattern.

'Rahul painted these walls,' my mother said. Gyani nodded with the same smile. Kumar looked on sullenly. 'He is a very artistic boy.'

He set down glasses of water and said, 'Here, Grease.'

I remembered my mother telling me that Kumar was never quite happy with Rahul, and that he was made to study hospitality management, or something like that, but mostly he played video games.

It was past three o'clock now, and Gyani made masala chicken, roti and paneer, pointing to each dish and carefully pronouncing each one. The family asked about our plans. Rahul's two sisters,

Geeta and Kavita, were giggling on either side of me. I leant back into the sofa, which was made of wood. Opposite was a small bed that looked just as hard. Gyani brought masala chai to the table. That was when Meenakshi arrived with her brother, Mak.

The whole family, I came to know, was from Kathmandu. We sat for several hours, talking about what we could do in New Delhi. I stayed out of the conversation most of the time, only nodding when my mother said, 'Wouldn't that be nice?' Geeta and Kavita were taking photos of themselves. Rahul had gone into another room. Gyani sat cross-legged next to Kumar. Mak was sitting beside him, listening. He had a pensive face. Meenakshi was talking about the night markets. We looked at each other in passing.

Three days later we were in Mumbai. Away from the cold and dirt of Delhi, it was hot now, and the streets were made of cobblestone. There were old Banyan trees all through the streets, and vines hung from the branches in clusters. The bricks laid around the trees had been pushed up by the roots, which often stretched to the street. The buildings were familiar, in the Victorian style, and the light looked yellow in the streets.

Outside the hotel, cows moved their muzzles around brick ruins in the alleyways, looking for food. We were staying in the Grand Hotel on the corner of Walchand Hirachand Marg and SS Ram Gulam Marg in the Ballard Estate. The square windows on the tower were arranged in an upwards winding shape. Behind the tower were two L-shaped buildings with four storeys. The courtyard in the centre was symmetrical like a Wes Anderson scene. A group of boys played cricket all afternoon in the street with slabs of wood and concrete. There was an old coffee house down the street, and outside the coffee house stray cats ran between the trees on the curb and underneath cars. A small black kitten with white socks looked at me from underneath a parked car.

I loved going in the old-style elevator and seeing the hotel floors, then walking down winding staircases and looking out each window. The doors were dark wood, and the doorknobs were brass. Coppersmith barbet birds were perched on the trees outside.

The dining room was always empty after the breakfast service and the waiters let me sit there to read whenever my mother was upstairs resting. I wanted to see the city, but I did not like to walk by myself – there were no women in the streets, only boys and staring men. So, I would sit, in a worn leather armchair at a small table. Dust came through the windows in with the light. Bicycle bells rang outside, and I heard the bell at the front desk as well as footsteps outside the frosted glass of the dining room. When I grew tired of reading, I tried to note down the things I had seen.

I started with the car ride to the Taj Mahal. I was thinking about how I hardly remembered it, with the family meeting us three hours late and then feeling so tired and sleeping in the car, and then finally getting to the Taj Mahal and being rushed through. But I left that out. Instead I wrote about how halfway to

Agra, somewhere near Jewar, we stopped at a food place off the highway. The floor was made of dirt and the cooks kneaded dough in front of huge tandoors. One man stood in front of the spices for the curries. I had about four cups of sweet masala tea, which cost only five rupees each, and ate dahl and rice with my fingers.

I wrote about how Geeta and Kavita brought a scarf for me to wear in photographs at the Taj Mahal. Meenakshi also gave me a tikka, and gold earrings with matching bangles to wear, and later she let me keep them. I wrote about seeing the Taj Mahal, a pure white marble creation against a grey-blue sky, but then about not really knowing what it was about after spending the time in photographs with the family. I wrote about the road back from the Taj Mahal at dusk, with monkeys swinging from the trees, baboons on rooftops, donkeys still pulling carts and oxen grazing on the roadside before a sky of dust and dying light.

I wrote about how the family made Rahul pretend to propose to me for a joke photograph and how they wanted me to look into his eyes as he knelt down. But something changed in his eyes. He became even stranger to me after that. He would leave the table as soon as he had finished eating and would not look at me. I didn't notice much because I spoke to Meenakshi instead.

I also wrote about Geeta, still in high school, and Kavita, married. I remembered one time the women of the family were joking about how it was unnecessary to be beautiful after getting married. The girls were asking about my literature degree when Kavita said to me, 'You are only expected to be married. You are raised to be married.' I said, 'Doesn't some kind of feminism exist here?' Geeta said 'No.' After a pause, I asked what they were studying in school. 'I like maths,' said Geeta. Kavita had finished high school but she said, 'I'm married.'

One calm time in the dining room, I wrote about the pigeons outside the hotel across the square before the Mumbai Gate, and how they looked like fruit hanging from the trees.

***

Back in Delhi, it was my birthday. We went with the family to a Chinese restaurant in Shahdara, the south-east region of Delhi. We had arranged that the family would come by the hotel at six o'clock and we would take the car together. They came at eight o'clock and Rahul was sleeping in the back. There was traffic to Shahdara, and it was nine o'clock before we got to the restaurant. When we got out and walked to the restaurant, the other boy of the family, Mak, was holding Rahul up by his shoulders. Beads of sweat had formed across his forehead, his eyes drooped, and his jacket was all wet down the front. At first, I thought he had fallen in water. But by the way everyone else was acting – the acted nonchalance of the young people, the ashamed and avoidant expressions of the parents – Rahul had taken something.

He sat next to me at the table and fell asleep quickly. Mak tried to laugh about it. Everyone drank wine or Coke. Meenakshi was drinking whiskey and I liked her even more. She was on my other side. I ordered a whiskey also.

'They are just different,' she said, about her previous boyfriend, a bartender.

'And they are always surrounded by girls,' I said, about mine.

'Yes, and they always flirt with them and then say, "it is just my job". But I think that's rubbish.'

'Me too,' I said. 'They are so confident but then you realise it is not true.'

'Yes, I think their insecurity, deep down, explains a lot.'

We were silent again then looked at each other and laughed, at the bartenders and then at talking about such things and suddenly falling silent. We took a drink.

'It is so strange that we can talk like this,' she said.

'Strange how?'

'Because I cannot talk like this with most people.'

'It is the same for me.'

Another silence.

'Do you know where the bathroom is?' I asked.

'No. But I'll go with you.'

The waiter pointed to the hallway down the right side of the restaurant.

'It is good to talk about sex with another girl,' she said, washing her hands. 'There is such stigma in India,' she continued. 'So many girls get pregnant because they go behind bushes with boys and don't understand what happens. And then they are shamed by their family.'

She told me about the first time she had been with a boy, and how he was forceful and shamed her afterwards.

She lifted herself onto the bathroom sink. She looked at me with careful eyes, like they were trying to uncover something buried far below the surface. It felt like she was gently brushing away the dust because she cared about what she might discover.

'It was the same with me. I was only thirteen. But it changed me.'

'I am sorry. Luckily, I was older. But still, I was raped.'

'I don't like that word. I don't ever like to say I was raped. That way, it is almost like it never happened.'

She nodded. The bathroom door opened. It was Geeta and Kavita.

'Oh, *there* you are. We have been looking for you.'

'We were just talking,' said Meenakshi. She slipped off the bathroom sink, landing silently on her toes. We should go, her eyes said to me. Kavita was in the bathroom and Geeta had started taking photos of herself.

'Come, take a photo with me,' said Geeta, staring into the camera and touching her hair, but we were already walking back.

At the table, everyone was talking as usual. Rahul's head was hanging off the back of the chair. There was a line of drool running down the side of his face. His father was the only other person who was not talking to someone else. He sat there, not touching the can of Coke, staring at Rahul, his face sagged with disgust and disappointment. Suraj patted Rahul on the back every so often, trying to make it all into a joke. But still it was very strange, and no one except Rahul's father seemed to care, although Suraj and Mak seemed knowing.

Meenakshi and I looked around at the table first, politely drinking. I put more food on my plate. She stared ahead with the short glass in her hand, before moving hair away from her face and speaking in a deeper tone. I think the whiskey did that.

'What helped me was using pain in sex.'

'You mean men would do it to you?'

'I did it to men. Powerful men. Men who were so powerful that they were begging to be treated like dogs and to be whipped.' She looked at me. 'It gave my power back to me.'

I nodded, thinking about it.

'Girls always feel sex is something being taken away from them, or we are giving something to the man,' she said.

We finished the whiskeys. The night was slowing down. The other conversations were finishing, and the food lay cold on the table. Rahul had his face in his plate of food. This night was truly strange. I wondered what it was all about and whether there was any meaning to it at all. Suraj pretended to laugh and patted him on the back again. Rahul's father stared at him with even greater distaste; the cracks were starting to show through. Yet through it all, I felt calm and clear in her company, as though we could talk without shame about the strangest and worst things we had ever done, our regrets and our pains and what we truly wanted out of life and it was like the other already knew. We could not talk as much with everyone else becoming quieter, but she leaned towards me so she could ask me something else.

'Have you ever done anything with girls?'

'No. I thought I would always feel safer with a girl, but I have never done anything. Although a girl kissed me once.'

She smiled at me.

'Have you?'

'Yes,' she said.

'What was it like?'

'I felt like myself.'

The waiters were clearing the table and the others were putting their jackets on. It was time to go.

I put my arm around my mother and said thank you for the dinner.

'It is nice to do something with everyone, right?'

'I don't know. But I liked talking to Meenakshi.'

'Yes, I saw. But still I am glad we had everyone here too.'

In the car home, I sat next to Meenakshi in the backseat with Rahul. Everyone was quiet. Rahul was still sleeping with his head back and his mouth open. He looked awful on the way to the car, his jacket still wet with whatever had been chucked up. Each time we drove past a streetlight, I saw the drool on his face.

'He will be sad without you,' joked Mak. Meenakshi was silent, looking out the window. Her head was resting on her hand.

Arriving at the Leela for what I realised would be the last time, everyone except Rahul got out to say goodbye.

'He will take you to the airport tomorrow morning,' said his father.

I was still in the back with Meenakshi. I was waiting for the seat to be pushed forward so I could also get out. She looked at me and said, 'It was very meaningful to me, our conversation.'

'For me also. I am glad we spoke.'

'If you like, I can come up with you. To your room. We can continue talking.'

She was looking at me in a certain way. I looked back and I felt my lips part slightly – they were suddenly dry. I pressed them back together to wet them before I spoke. There was a suggestion in her eyes now.

'I would like to. But I share the room with my mother.'

'Maybe next time,' she said with a small smile. She followed me out of the car.

We were standing to the side of everyone hugging goodbye.

'Could I have a kiss before you go?'

'Of course,' I laughed. I kissed her on the cheek. No one saw. She smiled sadly.

'You should try doing something, like what I said. I think it would be good for you.' I nodded. 'And tell me when you do!'

Geeta and Kavita came to say goodbye. I hugged them both. Meenakshi stood to the side, watching. I said goodbye to their parents, bowing my head and saying thank you, for what I wasn't sure, but they understood the respect. Suraj and Mak hugged me goodbye too. They all waved one last time and loaded back into the car.

'We will stay in touch,' I said to Meenakshi. She nodded again, sadly. She looked very beautiful under the warm lights of the Leela with her golden bangles catching the light.

'Please, can I have another kiss?'

Mother and I watched the car leave and walked into the hotel. The doormen bowed their heads to us, the yellow fringe on their hats swinging. I was tired and a bit drunk and feeling nostalgic about the trip. But I knew it was more about Meenakshi than anything else. I thought about her as I waited on the bed for my mother to finish showering and I fell asleep thinking of her sad, beautiful face outside the hotel. Why did these things always have to happen just before leaving?

Our flight left Delhi the next morning at nine o'clock. At six o'clock, we were in the lobby of the hotel waiting for the car to take us to the airport. Rahul never came.

***

At the café, my father had finished his coffee. I was pressing my fingers against the last crumbs of the carrot cake. The waitresses were wiping down tables.

'I've been reading the most fascinating things about *apsaras* lately.'

'The Indian nymphs?'

'You know about them?'

'You told me something about them once or twice. And also, there were some sculptures and paintings of them in the museums.'

'That's good that you went to see some.'

He continued to tell me all that he had learnt about *apsaras*, the stories and mythology and all the names. But as I listened, I only heard that the word itself comes from 'water', like the water in the clouds, and that *apsaras* were accomplished and beautiful nymphs divine.

TWINS

Anastasia Taig

Identical
like a second skin
or a mirrored face
reflected through the decades

It's seeing yourself at the cellular level
through the microscope of time
with reassuring double vision
that drills down to the bones

It is the knee-deep comfort
of knowing that life's currents
can never drag you under,
for you are steadied by a second self

And though you wrestle for the superficial
assurance of an individuality,

there is an exhaled breath of stillness
drawn from that ever-present Other –

The twin-split egg,
the refracted heart.

PARALYSIS

Anastasia Taig

They did this to me.

I move from a biography into abstraction
Each noun sonorous, each verb perverse.
But where else can I drink my fill
If not in language?

My legs dangle –
A bungee cord,
Umbilical, still slack
Quiescent.

I long for the blood rush,
The pulsing burn of air,
The letter proof of life.
Adrenalin like acid,
Like heroin.
I want the drug of movement.

But I am severed at the spine –
Sexless puppet on a wire
That dangles, impotent, above.

This useless body is a broken steeple:
It gathers blessed dust.

They give me parking spots and envelopes,
Say I can live a normal life.
How can I when they stole my body and my voice?
Even the words – clinical, sterile –
Are theirs, not mine.

All I can do
Is take their words,
Draw them deep into me, let them seed,
Gestate them
Give birth
Within another incarnation.

They want me genderless and mute
But letters hammer in my skull
Like morse code suffrage.
They claim my body and my voice,

My movement and my gender,
My art and science and design,
But I transcend their language
And I divide.

STORIES BEHIND OPERA CURATION

Jing Cai

As a Chinese person researching opera from a socio-cultural background rather than a musical one, I was often asked – why? Why *opera*? If I was not myself, I would probably not easily understand why. But I am myself, and I felt lost every time I was asked at the Conservatorium: 'What do you play?'

Many times, I thought I did not belong in the world of music, did not belong to the world of the West, and did not belong to the people who I have been working and living with. Loneliness crept up on me and I saw how strange I was among the crowd, just like the dramatic scene from the film, *Lost in Translation*. To start a new career and life in a new place is not easy, but I wasn't going to give up on being a part of the world I hadn't fully mixed in with yet. I continued my research and hoped it would change one day.

Things became different when I started interviews for my research in Beijing last year. I was trying to collect diverse opinions and suggestions on opera development from theatre leaders, composers, conductors, directors, singers and media professionals. In the process, I acquired a lot of valuable data, but there were three things that impressed me more deeply than the data: their ideals, their love, and their passion for opera. I found these things in each interviewee's face, tone and attitude, sparkling with emotion. I found them in each handshake, hug, and interaction, with belief and integrity. Between each recording, I suddenly understood what connected me to opera, and China to the world. It is not language, skin, or expertise, but unaffected ideals, love, and passion. The former identifies our social attributes, while the latter identifies our inherent power. It is the latter that determines possibility, and how much we can give to the world.

When I returned to Australia, I wanted to contain those ideals, the love and the passion I found in Chinese opera practitioners, potentially common in all human beings, in a crystal bottle. So, I launched a research exhibition, *Rising from the East: Opera in China*, at the Sydney Conservatorium of Music Library as a means of preservation. The exhibition was presented between 25 March and 25 May 2019, showing how Western-style operas are created and produced in China, with exhibits including video, audio, DVDs, books, programs, photos, scores, and costumes. It was organised in an operatic structure, with a three-act format. It started with familiar Western repertoire consisting of *Turandot*, *Die Fledermaus*, *Rigoletto*, *Aida* and *Der Fliegende Holländer* in Act 1, then focused on contemporary Chinese opera *Jinsha River* and *Visitors on the Snow Mountain* composed by Lei Lei

(雷蕾) in Act 2. Finally, it ended with important achievements of the National Centre for the Performing Arts (NCPA) in Beijing in Act 3. For many Westerners, this was the first time for them to have a visual sense of operatic culture in China. It turns out that China not only has traditional Chinese opera, but has also been a prosperous context for the survival and development of Western-style opera, stimulating people to explore a Western art form through a new cultural lens.

The contemporary Chinese opera, *Jinsha River*, composed by Lei Lei, was an important part of this exhibition. The opera is a fusion of Chinese regional music and Western operatic techniques, showing a unique blend of styles. I was asked many questions about Lei Lei during the exhibition period, including questions about her background, career, works, life and even her personality, far more than the exhibition showed. However, people's interests have self-explanatory reasons, which often motivate us to discover more stories.

Lei Lei used to be a very successful film and television music composer in China, with a number of famous songs to her name. I still remember the first time I met Lei Lei eight years ago; I wanted her autograph immediately for my mother because her music for the TV series *Ke Wang* (*Expectation*) was so popular and acclaimed among that generation. But in recent years, Lei Lei has shifted her career to become an almost full-time opera composer, and has completed seven operas in total: *Xishi*, *The Chinese Orphan*, *Visitors on the Snow Mountain*, *Jinsha River*,

Wu Zetian, *Liu Sanjie* (*Third Sister Liu*) and *The Red Army Is Not Afraid of The Expedition*.

As to the reason she made this transition, she explained it in the words of Zuohuang Chen (陈佐湟), China's celebrated conductor: 'Once you start opera composition, you would not be willing to work on film and television music anymore.' Since she started her first opera, she has declined most commissions for film and television music because she is so addicted to opera; an art form which channels all her ideas, talents and passion into something really sublime. She believes that no composer can refuse the opportunity to create opera. When I interviewed Lei Lei at her home in Beijing, her husband, Ming Yi (易茗), lyricist and librettist, also joined our discussion. They are always the strongest supporters of each other and have collaborated on many songs and a few operas. As the interview went on, they occasionally argued on some questions with differing opinions, but it revealed some lovely moments of both demanding artists, and an ordinary happy couple.

Lei Lei's career, to a large extent, demonstrates the rising operatic environment in China today. Behind the phenomenon is the rapid development of theatre culture, the performance industry, and opera production in China, that enables composers like Lei Lei to have more choices to work on opera instead of popular music. My interviews found that the NCPA, inaugurated in December 2007, was commonly considered one of the most important factors in developing opera culture in China.

My exhibition explored this national theatre and its effective strategies.

A valuable exhibit piece was the book *Theatre Operation Management: The National Centre for the Performing Arts Model of Structuring*, which is the first of its kind in China on theatre operation and management, written by Ping Chen (陈 平), the first president of the NCPA. He is a miraculous figure in my mind, always making the impossible, possible. Sometimes I'd ask myself, if I had an opportunity to run a grand theatre from its birth, what would the theatre become in ten years' time? That was an extremely difficult question for me, but a job well done by Ping Chen. More importantly, he has recorded and theorised his unique practice and experience in his book, so that the success of the NCPA can be learnt or replicated by other theatres, making consistent contributions to China and the world.

The NCPA is a huge arts centre consisting of four theatres. The building has an oval shape, like an egg or a pearl floating on the water, so people nicknamed it the 'giant egg'. This is not the most elegant name for an art centre, which to some extent suggests that the extremely expensive 'egg' was not expected by most people to incubate anything great at the beginning. Theatre culture hadn't formed in China, and it would be a challenge to run a theatre on such a large scale. However, the NCPA has survived and was managed successfully under Ping Chen's leadership. In particular, his strategy of opera production enabled the NCPA to deeply connect China and the world, stimulating the opera industry worldwide. Just a few days before I interviewed Ping Chen in Beijing, he received a letter from conductor Zubin Mehta and his wife, old friends of the NCPA, so I was very fortunate to know some of the contents of this letter:

> I praise you all around the world for your wisdom, your high standards, your great achievements, and your wise leadership of the NCPA. The productions that you, as a representative of China, have presented are world-class and unique. No language can express my praise to you. I hope that your government will fully realise that what you have created for China will contribute to the precious wealth of the future. You are such an outstanding model.

Ping Chen's leadership extends across many fields, including art, culture, management, business, and city administration. In his career and life, he has experienced many moments of transition, but I think his name will be inseparable from the NCPA because he developed the theatre from an infant into a real giant. All his ideals are there as the principles he made for the NCPA, 'for the people, for art, for the world'.

While preparing for the exhibition, I got a chance to see a few documentaries filmed in the early years of the NCPA. At that time, Ping Chen looked so inspirational, with black hair. Now, he is still inspirational, but black hair has turned to grey. Somehow, with tears in my eyes, I am not sure whether it was the theatre that stole the man's time, or that the man has exchanged his time for the growth of the theatre.

Space is always limited for displaying things, but memory isn't. When I collected objects for the exhibition, I was collecting the stories behind the objects and finding the common spirit from these stories. Lei Lei and Ping Chen are only two of many opera practitioners in China. They have devoted themselves to the opera, an art form integrating both Chinese and Western cultures, through which they may find themselves in the international arena, not because of their language, skin or expertise, but because of their works, their talents and their innovations.

Although the exhibition is about 'opera in China', it contains more than opera and China alone. When I was conducting interviews in Beijing, Chinese practitioners were also eager to know about opera in Australia. So, opera produced by different countries may have different features, but I believe, as do opera practitioners and researchers, that the ideals, the love and the passion for opera is the same. We hope good things will remain, be inherited, and develop wherever they are.

The exhibition has ended, but for me it never ends because there are so many people who have contributed to the exhibition in different ways. Operatic practitioners, librarians, academics, musicians, technicians, teachers and classmates – they made me believe that I have always been a part of them, and not a stranger in the world anymore.

ANYWHERE, EVERYWHERE

Sarah Poh

Over the water, green-grey like the map of veins on his arm, our guide had held out a bucket as red as the raw meat it contained. The boat engine had ceased, and a hushed silence had fallen upon us. This is perhaps the only memory I have of Langkawi.

We were flanked by cliff faces and dense thickets and my knuckles had turned taut on the life vest. I clung onto it despite my dissipating confidence in its ability to keep me alive. Knocking the bucket against the boat's hull in rapid succession, the guide had let out a strangely mellifluous whistle. I doubted I had ever been that alert. Who knows, I could have been the next contributor to a horrific video of a wildlife tour gone wrong.

In retrospect, that might have been the first time after the funeral that I had paid my surroundings due attention. I realised then, that my will to live was much stronger than I'd thought. That I mustn't have been as depressed as I'd thought I was, or maybe, when faced with the very possibility of losing your life, it simply becomes that much more desirable.

Chunks of red meat flew. Flung from the bucket, they were caught by two swooping shadows before they touched the water.

I've lost many things in my lifetime. But my greatest loss is you.

***

Long red candles bleeding next to piles of golden *joss* paper. Just like the ones at your funeral. The unrelenting, biting winds that plagued the imperial garden had forced me within the temple walls. I remember drawing closer to the flames, its incense intoxicating. I had nearly seen you again, organising the abundant food offerings on the altar, which you kept cleaner than your bedroom. My hands and feet were as frozen as the lakes in Beijing's Forbidden City and I wished the ache in my chest had frozen, too. Folding a *joss* paper into an ingot, just as you taught me, I knelt, watching the flames devour the offering into ashes.

I still haven't gone back to where yours lie.

I wish the ache in my chest would melt.

It was almost as if we couldn't bring ourselves to step out of our bubbles of grief, enlarging them by only being around each other, all the time, like how bubbles coalesce upon contact. I used to join the oil globules atop the soup you made, while waiting for it to cool. Now I see that we'd decided to run as far and as long as our finances had permitted when the bubble burst and asphyxiation's grip became overwhelming.

The pear soup at hawker stalls never tastes as good as yours.

***

Fine white powder blanketed the landscape. I wondered what it felt like to be buried six feet under all those layers. On the way up the mountain, I had sunk into it knee-high, the sensation forcing a hyper-awareness of my movements.

The Tokyo boy I had met in Sydney came to mind – more precisely, his baffled expression at the fact that I would be visiting his country, but not the mainland. It had seemed unfathomable to him why anyone would be more interested in the least developed island of Japan, rather than the city he hailed from.

It felt like icing sugar.

Winters in Hokkaido are not as harsh as they are made out to be. I withdrew my hand back into the room and contented myself with staring at the faint yellow glow of a distant streetlamp peering through the curtain of snow. At that moment, I was no longer simply going through the motions, as I had become so accustomed to doing ever since you left.

I remember the growing sense of serenity – unfamiliar, elusive, welcomed, precious. Relief.

ECOTONE

Sofia Ahmad

I am the river that flows between two worlds,
From the warm, sun-stained homes of Karachi,
To the too-cool breeze of Sydney's beaches.
I come from rope beds with hammocks tied underneath
Now resting upon brand-new mattresses with comforters on top.

I am the ebb and flow that link these two strange worlds.
I am not one, nor the other, but neither and both.
I am the dark-haired *dulhan* covered in her scarlet *dupatta,*
While humming the tune of 'Here Comes the Bride'.

I am the late-night McDonalds burger runs,
While Mum grumbles about having biryani at home.
I am memories of wearing *mehndi* to school the day after Eid,
And reminding myself to call it henna when people ask.

I am speaking to aunties in broken Urdu, with English littered
in between,
And I am the delight of finding old Bollywood movies on Netflix.

I am a heretic, connecting two mismatched places that had never been connected
And as my water flows, gently guiding my two homes together,
The world thanks me for it.

A PARADOX OF SEA AND COAL

Gabrielle Cadenhead

An Ode to Newcastle's Beaches

Red-bellied black ships haunt the horizon,
anchors sunk teeth-deep,
tethering seabed to sky.
                Sea breeze tinged with serpent breath –
they pierce the picturesque
with bellies hungry for coal.

Red-bellied black ships stalk the horizon.
We count
        the twenty-something reptiles
                to be cropped from postcards,
and fail
                to intervene
        between serpent and sea.

Furnaced by fossil breath,
the sand scorches our soles.

We count and they wait,
while around us
venom seeps into the sea.

DIVERSITY? NOT SO MUCH HERE

Cherita Zhu

Linka Tide came into university earlier than usual that Monday. She sat in the library at her customary place on Level 1, reviewing her slide show for her marketing presentation due at 3 pm that day. Her group had already emailed her their components. She was responsible for reviewing all the materials and putting the cumulative research neatly into a powerpoint.

She was not excited for this presentation, nor was she weary yet – she had done countless of them before in junior units for her marketing degree. She was not frightened by public speaking and didn't doubt her group members. They were studying combined degrees at the University of Sydney and were in their penultimate or final year.

Linka added the final clip art pieces to the first slide of the presentation and checked that all of their student numbers were on the powerpoint's file name. It took a long time for her to save up for this laptop, whichwas already slightly dirty from the leftover juice on her fingers from the grapes she had eaten on her way to campus.

When the time came to present, Linka and her two group

members were on the dot with the twelve-minute time limit. In their corporate attire and black enclosed shoes, they looked the part for the recommendations on an expansion plan that they had chalked out for the Panadol company and were responsible for 'selling' to the tutor and class – a class that peered at them from above their own laptops.

The subject of marketing – the specific specialisation that focused on medical streams of marketing and the ethics behind the dream media case, for any consulting company really – occupied her thoughts.

Panadol is a traditional over-the-counter drug sold to help soothe pain. At first, it was administered as a sugary syrup to the delight of slightly confused children. Only when fast-paced, shorter time-out breaks during a school sports game became compulsory, Panadol evolved into a white pill to be swallowed without much thought.

Linka's auburn hair tickled her ears as she grabbed Panadol a few weeks later from the top of her father's bedside table. Linka's father, Mr Tide, was a quiet, bald man who once had brown hair. He seldom spoke except for 'Can we fix it?', 'Yes we can!' Bob the Builder-esque conversations. His appearance was always tidy, especially on church Sundays. Mrs Tide was from the class of the 1980s, a debutante at the high school Linka had attended. Though, in her bedside table's lamp light, her ample wrinkles reflected her age quite clearly. At every school hall assembly and celebration she still came across as a very beautiful woman.

Linka opened the lid of her Mount Franklin water bottle for the first time and drank from it. She popped the pill from its silver packet, choosing one at random, for they were all manufactured the same, and put it on her tongue and drank some more water to help it go down. Looking forward to the summer break when Matt would soon be free to go to Souls, Linka checked her Sydney University email account and felt nothing at her final mark.

Matt was a man who was not that interested in the details of Linka's study at the University of Sydney for he was a part-time engineer at Schneider Electric and also in his final year of his double degree here at Sydney. Matt had brown hair with the most brilliant blue eyes and a tendency to carry his brown leather satchel every time he left his home. Linka and Matt had met at a university social and Linka spilt her wine on Matt. Linka was wearing a sequined number so she was honestly not that upset that Matt was the one who got the red liquid on his white-collared shirt, as her darling charcoal dress meant a lot to her. It was a night in September and it meant much to many, not just them, meeting for the first time. By the end of the fashion parade the girls, including Stacy and Lauve, were successful in being the stars of photos taken by the photographers of the night as they donned the most extravagant 1920s costumes and bright pink feather boas challenging the neutral-hue 'Drama Girls' norm.

Unimpressed by her own actions, Linka Tide did not do much of the talking and so the spill on Matt's shirt was solved almost immediately by the wait staff at the Vista Ballroom who were responsible for the catering of the university event. Stacy was also a marketing major and one of Linka's best friends and was wearing a red fluffy tube dress and electric blue eyeliner. Linka felt tired and tried to leave the venue asap. However, it was Stacy who pulled Matt and Linka together, and with a new cup of the finest red each, they sat and talked deeply into the night.

The final mark Linka received for the marketing assignment was a sixty-eight. Lauve felt that the university was a mad cow, suffering from a disease difficult to get over, with its pristine facilities and polished head business leaders. Linka thought the animal reference was because of Lauve's all too helpful carrying of the dirty dinner plates at the close of the university event.

Linka felt nothing at her final mark. Linka carried the Panadols in their silver foil trays to her chosen work experience place for the summer break, as Souls was cancelled by Matt at the last minute. With her parents, Mr and Mrs Tide, not feeling a thing when Matt and all his brown chocolate warmth disappeared upon hearing of Linka's complacent attitude towards her university studies. They had also grown apart as they learnt more about each other and saw the petty yet super picky and deal-breaker parts they did not admire in each other's skin and bone. They saw faults in each other, more than the popular in the early 2010s book *The Fault in our Stars* by John Green, and it got to the point that even the Panadol (now deemed special a semester after Linka's marketing assignment) and their drowsy effect had a much more serene meaning to Linka's eighteen-turning-nineteen-year-old life than men like Matt and their white business shirts. The Panadol stayed in Linka's Victoria's Secret metallic-pink makeup pouch, even when Mr Yoon (Matt) was out with his leather satchel, the iconic thing replaced by his sister who had noticed that the carrying strap was fraying and fragile with age.

مُحَمّدْ رياض عَوَاد

Mohammad Awad

Zaatar manoushe, منقوشة زعتر
Kaak with cheese, كعك بجبن
Lebanese *Shay,* شاي لبنان

Call it *Shoy* شاي
with my country Arab twang

Into your home.

You prefer
English Breakfast.

You pronounce my name
as a stutter,
An echo of my mother's first word,
My father's prayer,

You know me as a suffix.

You make no real effort,
attempts are flaccid.

My name would bring
Choirs to your ear canals,
Religious experiences
onto the rolls of your tongue,
Would invoke
the word of God الله
in its whisper,
make *Zamzam* زمزم
out of the beer
In your breath,

My apologies
Jake,

I don’t know how to make you care
about hearing your Love
Say your name.

Mohammad Riad مُحَمَّدْ رياض
Awad عَوَاد

ASSIMILATION

Mary Stanley

Holographic warfare shimmered across the lounge room wall as blindingly white hands hurried to reload a rifle. Ferris was sprawled on the couch in his underwear, fingers mashing his game controller. Static pricked his corneas and his eyelids were heavy, but he resisted and kept playing.

Gunfire and fleshy splatters blared from the speakers. Blood sprayed across the projected scene, momentary red light peppering the furniture and Ferris's bare legs. A half-finished protein shake and last night's stale potato chips sat abandoned on the coffee table.

Ferris cursed and sat up, elbows on his knees, eyes fixed on the hologram. His fingers blurred as he played. Bullets ripped into an ectomorphic black android and blue crackles of electricity lit up the darkened lounge room. He laughed and sat back against the couch.

'Suck it, fool.'

Garvey ambled out into the lounge room, red light sliding across his slim pearlescent face and forearms. He set his amber eyes on Ferris, then turned into the kitchenette with a scoff. An in-game explosion burst from the speakers, rattling the knick-knacks on the entertainment unit.

Garvey clapped his hands over his ears. He stalked over and snatched the remote off the coffee table and lowered the volume with a quick swipe.

'It's six in the morning, Ferris. Just 'cause you're up doesn't mean the rest of the world has to be.'

Ferris rolled his glazed, blue eyes. Garvey dropped the remote onto the coffee table and headed to the kitchenette. Ferris spoke to someone on his neural link in his sharp Exfractian dialect. The informal vulgarity made Garvey grind his teeth. He turned and looked at Ferris.

'What?' Ferris shrugged.

'Do you have to talk like that?'

'Like what?'

'Never mind.'

Groaning, Garvey pulled a soggy box out of the sink and threw it to the side. It hit the three days' worth of dishes and empty packets of microwave dinners that were littered all over the counter.

'Why haven't you *cleaned* anything?'

'Wait, hold on, Bishop. What, Garvey?'

'You've been up since –'

'I've been at work all week,' Ferris looked away from the projection.

'So, have I! You could've done –'

'Most of that shit is yours. Why should I clean up your mess?'

It *was* Garvey's mess; Ferris' body didn't have a digestive system. Whatever he did eat, he would throw up within the hour. Garvey inhaled and turned on the tap, the argument wasn't worth it. Water gushed out onto the dishes and bounced off, spraying him. He turned off the tap, kneading the palms of his hands into his eyes.

Ferris swiped a fingertip against his temple to turn off game connectivity and the white film over his eyes dissipated. He heaved himself up off the lounge and entered the kitchenette to stand beside Garvey.

'How're you feeling?'

'Like shit, Ferris.'

'Alright, don't be so anal,' Ferris distanced himself. 'You need to stop taking –'

'It's not the dionide.'

'It is. I don't need that shit, no one does.'

'Yeah, it's easier for you, you don't need to sleep.'

Ferris shrugged. 'Hey, you wanted all the human functions, you got them. I was picky about what I got.'

Garvey rolled his amber eyes. 'Being poor is not the same as being picky.'

'Yeah, thanks for reminding me.'

Garvey chucked the empty packages into the bin under the sink. Ferris drew in a breath and slipped in front of Garvey. He couldn't stand him pouting.

'Sit down, I'll make coffee and clean up here.' Ferris began rinsing leftover scraps off the dishes. Garvey opened his mouth to protest but Ferris waved him off. 'Go, man.'

Garvey hobbled over to the couch and dropped onto the cushions. Ferris started scrubbing dishes in the sink. When he looked over at Garvey, the other android was already asleep. Head tipped back, the wheeze of overworked engines and batteries came from his open mouth.

***

Garvey jolted awake. Gunfire. Softer this time, the volume turned down. He groaned and stretched, spine cracking. Ferris was fixated on the violent hologram projected on the wall. He was wearing all black activewear, too tight around his muscled chest and thighs, camouflaging him in the dark. Ferris appeared strikingly human upon first glance, but not so much the second. He almost fooled Garvey when they'd first met on a night out, but his abnormal height and blacked-out sclera were a dead giveaway.

Before Ferris left Exfracta, he paid a hefty sum to have genitalia constructed for him, hair plugs implanted in his skull, and a chip hammered into his spine. The chip stimulated hair and muscle growth and changed his charcoal skin to sun-kissed olive.

Garvey sat up and rubbed his face. A stone-cold coffee on a plastic coaster awaited him. He reached for it and Ferris grunted, still watching the projection.

'It's pond water now. I'll make another one.'

‘It’s fine, I don’t want to waste it.’

‘There’s a big packet of the synthetic stuff left.’

Garvey took a sip of his coffee, fighting off a grimace. ‘I don’t like that one.’

‘What’s wrong with it?’

‘The organic stuff is better.’

‘It costs, like, thirty dollars more.’

‘So?’

‘Alright, your highness,’ Ferris’ thumbs stabbed at the controller buttons.

His character took damage and died, the hologram flashing red. He scoffed and relaxed back against the lounge, expression souring. Half asleep, Garvey took a slow slurp of his coffee.

‘Why do you keep playing this?’

‘It’s fun. I’ve made some friends on here too.’

‘Don’t you find it weird that the humans made this game and the majority of the players are, you know, our kind?’

‘No, they’ve been playing shooting games like this for centuries.’

Ferris started a new game. The character selection screen displayed a carousel of sleek white androids with glowing orange eyes holding pulse rifles and laser spears. Ferris’ character was dropped into a metropolitan sprawl to hunt blocky grey androids.

‘You’re killing your own caste.’

‘They’re not, they’re – it doesn’t matter, you don’t play –’

'No, seriously, that's all it is. What's so good about killing *ser* –'

'I don't know, why don't you ask your family?'

Ferris didn't look at Garvey when he said it; he knew what Garvey's expression was. Cold, pinched like he'd been slapped.

'We're not going there.'

'You started it,' Ferris said through his teeth. 'Just let me play, alright.'

Garvey took in a shallow breath and chose not to fight. He propped his head against the back of the lounge and closed his eyes.

'You should probably go to the doctors, man,' Ferris said.

'I can't afford that right now,' Garvey shook his head.

'Don't worry, I'll pay.'

'With the money you don't have, yeah, okay.'

'You just need to get off the pills and –'

'Fuck, enough already. I'll stop, just not now, okay?' Garvey pinched the bridge of his nose.

Ferris raised his hands in surrender, then went back to playing. Garvey headed into the kitchenette with his cup. He downed his coffee and rinsed out the coffee grounds. As he passed the fridge, the calendar caught his eye. He stepped back and looked at Ferris' handwriting scrawled under the date.

'We've got an appointment at Intercon today.'

'Shit, I knew I was forgetting something,' Ferris grumbled, hanging his head. 'Is all the paperwork and stuff ready?'

'Yes, it's on my desk. I'll go get dressed.'

Garvey rushed to get ready. Ferris swiped his temple, switching off his game. He left the controller on the couch and cracked his knuckles. The lounge room was dark save for the faint blue glow of his eyes.

***

The train into Redfern was packed despite it being the slowest, oldest form of travel. It was the cheapest option after all. It took about two hours to get into the city. Intense summer heat filled the carriages, the passengers' clothes all drenched in sour sweat.

Ferris pressed himself into the corner by the exit doors and wrapped an arm around Garvey's shoulders, covering the other android's eyes with his palm. A massive bang cut the air as the train clattered through a tunnel. Ferris closed his eyes just as the carriage interior went dark.

Garvey flinched awake and groaned. The train left the tunnel and sunlight blinded them. As Garvey moved, Ferris dropped his arm around the shorter android's waist.

'Where are we?' Garvey mumbled.

'Almost there, get ready,' Ferris scanned the sardined carriage. 'It'll be a fight to get out of here.'

Garvey yawned and cracked his neck. The train pulled up to the platform, doors facing a weathered brick shelter. Garvey smoothed his clothes and turned to the doors, Ferris behind him.

Air wheezed out of the carriage as the doors cracked apart. Chatter exploded around them as the passengers spilled onto the platform. It took five minutes to climb the stairs, another five to get through the turnstiles in the station.

The crowd flowed out onto Lawson Street. Ferris kept his arm around Garvey, it was too easy to lose one another in the flood of pedestrians. Busted old cars lined the street bumper to bumper, drivers honking and swearing. Construction vehicles clamoured behind the brick wall of fading art. Young students hurried west, a barrage of colourful ads and notifications flickering across the curd-white lenses in their eyes.

Ferris stood at the edge of the gutter and looked out. Heaving metal skyscrapers grew out of the horizon. Smog blanketed the rooftops, the sky near indistinguishable from the silver cityscape. Behind the polluted clouds, the sun glowed a stale yellow.

Ferris comically waved the air into his nose and puffed out his chest. A mixture of stinging chemical spills and industrial fumes clogged his airways.

'Ah, just like the slums back home.'

Chuckling, Garvey patted Ferris' shoulder, urging him to follow. They headed down the street, towards Intercon.

Ferris and Garvey manoeuvred around the construction sites squeezing the perimeter of Intercon. Traffic on the old road was immovable and verbal abuse, drilling, and beeping buzzed around their heads. There was the occasional crackling of metals being welded into place, the stench of burning steel saturating the air.

Ferris spied some androids working on the construction

sites. Their naked charcoal and silver frames glimmered under orange warning lights. He waved at them. They almost waved back. *Almost*. They turned away upon seeing Garvey beside him. Ferris lowered his hand and kept walking.

Intercon was a rigid one-storey building wedged between budding skyscrapers and elevated highways made of Exfractian metals. It was painted a depressing grey with a white lemniscate logo, like two clover leaves, above the sliding doors.

Dirt and fingerprints clouded the glass and the doors whined as they slid open. The android security guard nodded when Ferris walked inside, Garvey in tow. Intercon's interior was painted hospital white and furnished with the bare minimum.

There were no free seats in the waiting area. People leaned against the walls or sat on the floor. Ferris stepped up to the admission screens and input their information with his knuckle. A numbered receipt slipped out and Ferris snatched it up.

'When's our appointment?' Garvey asked.

'Doesn't matter,' Ferris shrugged, 'they're always fuckin' late.'

'How long is the wait going to be?'

Ferris examined the crowd in the waiting area. He chewed his lip.

'Hours.'

They headed over to the phone booths and took a seat, facing the waiting area. The humans there veered away from extra-terrestrials of any sort; their eyes unnaturally focused on the floor or the walls, bodies hunched away from any alien presence.

Ferris took the phone down and held it to his ear. He put on a high-pitched nasal accent and spoke into the receiver.

'Greetings –'

Garvey took the phone and placed it back on the hanger. 'C'mon, not here.'

'I'm just messin' around.'

'Well, don't. They'll find any excuse to kick us out.'

Ferris arched in his seat and whined, 'What am I meant to do, man? It's so boring in here, I'm gonna explode from ... boredom.'

'You're not the only one here,' Garvey countered. 'We've got to be patient.'

'Patience isn't in my programming,' Ferris stood. 'I'll get lunch from Fatman's.'

'It's going to be dinner by the time you get back.'

'Do you want anything, yes or no?'

'Just get the usual,' Garvey waved at Ferris.

'Alright,' Ferris nodded and deepened his voice, adding an accent, '*I'll be back.*'

He clicked his tongue and gave a thumbs up. Smiling, Garvey watched him strut out of Intercon.

'Garvey. *Garvey!*'

Garvey jolted awake and sat bolt upright in his seat. Still at Intercon, with Ferris standing over him, shaking him awake.

'Shit,' Garvey groaned and rubbed his eyes.

'You're passing out everywhere now, you really need to go

to the doctors.' Ferris handed him a polystyrene take-away container.

'I'm fine.'

'You're not fine. We're going to the medical centre after this.'

An Intercon worker in smart office attire approached the waiting area. She looked around and called out a ticket. No one claimed the number. Whoever had it probably already left, frustrated by the delay. The worker returned to her office. Ferris spied four people working, two of which were chatting to one another and laughing at images on their screens.

He bit into his kebab and chewed. His body whined and tried to process the food. It threated to come up, but he jabbed his fist against his sternum and forced the food to go down.

'I don't know why you bother eating,' Garvey wiped sauce away from his mouth, 'you keep making yourself sick.'

'Gotta keep up appearances,' Ferris replied, peeling the wrapping off his kebab.

'Everyone here knows what you are,' Garvey said. He continued, correcting himself, 'We're not exactly fooling anyone.'

'Yeah, but they like you,' Ferris cut back. 'You're rich and civilised.'

'That doesn't mean anything,' Garvey's voice was soft.

The Intercon worker returned. 'Number 604.'

Ferris patted Garvey's knee. 'That's us.'

The pair fumbled to rewrap food and close take-away boxes.

Garvey gathered their paperwork. The Intercon worker led Ferris and Garvey away to her office.

The office was all white save for the black screen built into the desk and the grey frosted glass door. There was a red laser on the worker's side of the desk. Crumbs and grease marks covered the workstation. Ferris peered at the screen and saw several active apps and online shopping tabs open.

'What can I do for you?' the Intercon worker asked, minimising the tabs as she sat down.

Garvey laid the documents on the desk. 'Our payments were recently cancelled, and I've submitted the paperwork to fix the issue about three times now – online and physically – but we haven't got our payments back.'

The Intercon worker scanned the barcodes at the top of every document. A moment of silence passed as she reviewed the information on the screen, feigning consideration. She clicked her tongue.

'According to the system, you were transferred from immigrant benefits to joint low-income middle of last year.'

Ferris slid a letter across the desk. 'Yeah, we're citizens now.'

The Intercon worker stared at Ferris. He scrunched his nose at her. Garvey kicked his foot under the desk.

'The system was re-evaluated in February, and joint low income is no longer an option. You were both transferred to low-income status but, based on the information provided about your respective incomes,' the Intercon worker continued, smiling,

'You're both earning above the threshold, so you don't qualify for Intercon payments.'

'What?' Ferris snapped.

'Ferris, let me talk,' Garvey hissed.

Ferris sat back, seething. Garvey shifted in his seat, sitting forward to look the Intercon worker in the eye.

'I'm sorry, but how are we earning above the threshold, exactly? Together, we're earning roughly a grand per week.'

The Intercon worker cocked her head. 'I'm sorry, but the low-income system is based on separate incomes. So, if I calculate –'

'We're both earning $487.92. Let's just move along.'

Garvey stared Ferris down. Ferris backed off, shutting his mouth.

Garvey sighed. 'Is there any kind of subsidy we can receive to help us?'

Ferris pinched the bridge of his nose; wrong question to ask. The Intercon worker appeared vexed, then shook her head. She smiled in a way that made Ferris want to spit on her.

'Sorry, but you're already living in Affordable Housing, so I don't think you need to receive further subsidies. Maybe if you take up another job, or work more hours, it would be easier for you.'

Ferris rolled his eyes. 'Seriously?'

The Intercon worker cocked a manicured eyebrow, face still fixed with that smug smile. Ferris widened his eyes.

'What? That's your only solution?'

'I've done all I can –'

'Bullshit.'

'Ferris.'

'Sir, you'll have to watch your language.'

Ferris leaned forward and sneered, his Exfractian accent slipping out on harder consonants, 'We work two factory jobs, ten, twelve hours a day, and we can barely afford our rent. We get paid fucking peanuts because we're not "qualified" even though where we're from, anyone can do low-level "engineering" shit. It's programmed into us right out of the gate and –'

'Sir, I understand –'

'No, you don't –'

'*Ferris.*'

'You get overpaid to sit on your arse six hours a day to tell all those poor bastards out there,' Ferris pointed over his shoulder, eyes still on the Intercon worker, 'that helping them survive is such a burden on the system!'

'Stop,' Garvey dug his fingers into Ferris' thigh.

Under the table, the Intercon worker pressed a button. Above the office door, a red light flicked on and a short buzzer sounded.

Ferris pushed Garvey's hand away. They exchanged a look and Garvey knew, in that moment, Ferris felt slighted by him, by his high caste. Garvey propped his elbow onto the arm of the chair, cradled his head in his hand.

'I'm sorry, but I have done everything that I can –'

'Oh, shut up, *cana*. You haven't done anything besides annoy me,' Ferris snarled, flicking his wrist. 'I've built machines smarter than you to clear shit from gutters. C'mon, Garvey, let's go.'

Ferris gathered their documents and stood up. Garvey let out a tight breath through his nose and kneaded his fingers against his forehead. The burly silhouettes of two security guards appeared beyond the frosted glass.

***

There was a burst of sound as Ferris and Garvey stumbled out of Intercon. Ferris swore at the security guards heading back into the building. Fuming, Garvey was already halfway down the street. Ferris jogged to catch up to him.

'Garvey –'

'You just can't shut up, can you?'

'Oh, c'mon, she was doing all that shit on purpose.'

'So what? We could've tried another way to –'

'What part are you missing, man? They're all like that!' Ferris gripped Garvey's shoulders, looking him straight in the eye. 'They don't care about how someone else is doing. Look at 'em.'

Ferris gestured to the surrounding crowds in the street. Some people marched with their heads up, looking forward, militant. Others were too fixated on what was behind their white lenses to notice. There was a jarring absence of conversation and interaction.

'They don't even like each other, and you reckon they'll like us?' Ferris questioned, navy pupils shrinking.

Garvey shook him off, avoided the intensity of his gaze. 'You should've just shut your mouth. I would've dealt –'

'Yeah, I can see how you dealt with it.'

'What, you did better by opening your big mouth?' Garvey bared his teeth.

'It didn't matter what we said or what paperwork we brought, she'd decided what she was gonna do before we even got in there.'

'That's not the point.'

'Then what –'

'You embarrassed me in there.'

'Oh, it's always –'

'*You embarrassed me*, Ferris,' Garvey repeated. He brought his hand between them, pointed a finger and continued. 'I warned you while we were in there, and you kept going. You didn't even listen to me –'

'Don't talk to me like I'm your *servero*,' Ferris' jaw set tight as he stood over Garvey, his tone poison. 'Everywhere we go, it's always you that's gotta handle things. Do you think I'm dumb or something?'

Garvey groaned, rolling his eyes. 'We're not doing this now.'

He turned and walked up the street. Ferris pursed his lips and drew a breath in through his nose.

'Oh, yes we are,' he hissed, trudging after the other android.

He moved through the crowd and caught Garvey at the intersection. There was a fluorescent orange pill bottle in Garvey's hand, the cap flipped open.

'Really, Garvey? How'd you even get that past me?'

Garvey was about to tip a capsule out when Ferris jabbed forward and snatched the bottle out of his fingers.

'Hey!'

'Enough of this shit.'

The two androids wrestled for the bottle. Garvey tried to wrench it back, but Ferris held on with a death grip. The orange plastic popped inside Ferris' fist and the dionide pills burst out, sprinkling the pavement.

Shocked, Garvey and Ferris looked down at the purple pills scattered across the concrete. The passing crowd crushed them into dust. Garvey's head snapped up, red fury flooding his eyes. He pushed Ferris and knocked him back a few steps.

'What the *fuck*?'

Garvey stomped past Ferris, shoulders bumping, and disappeared into the crowd. Ferris chucked the empty pill bottle into the gutter. A whistle came from the construction site next to him.

Three other Exfractians sidled up to the chain-link fence. Their patchwork high-vis uniforms were smeared with dirt and spotted with orange bleach stains. They were barefoot, no need for shoes. No need for clothes either, but it was out of courtesy, modesty, for the humans.

The leader of the group was taller and bulkier than the others, with a blocky torso made for lifting and firm stout legs for holding his ground. His rigid hands were scraped raw, revealing the factory-set grey metal underneath. A dated industrial heavy, probably a thousand years older than Ferris.

Smirking, the leader greeted, 'Hey, *servero*.'

'Don't call me that,' Ferris started walking.

'That's what you are, no?' The leader's accent was thick, clumsily rolling on the *r*'s and cutting short on the vowels. 'You're no *regio*, and you're not human either. What do you think you are?'

Ferris tried to ignore him, but the entourage followed him down the street. The leader's head blocked out the pale sunlight. The two other androids chattered in Exfractian. Ferris understood them – it was his dialect – and tried to ignore what he knew. Irritation prickled at the back of his neck.

'You might like that *regio* back there, but he don't like you. Doesn't matter if you're here, or on Exfracta, you two will never get along.'

'Don't talk to me like you know me,' Ferris shook his head, not looking at the leader.

'You and me? Same. But you and him will always be different,' the leader gestured as he spoke. 'Don't hurt yourself trying to be his equal. He's *regio*, you're *servero*, that's how it will always be, at least to him.'

Ferris stopped and stared up at the leader of the entourage. 'Me and you are different. I didn't leave Exfracta to be a *servero* to the cavemen here too.'

The leader's nose scrunched, and he gave Ferris a cold look. He spat on the pavement and cursed in Exfractian. The leader gestured to the entourage and they trailed off to chitter in their slum caste dialect. Ferris bowed his head and headed up the street, trying to contact Garvey. Texts and calls were left on seen, not blocked. Ferris stopped trying as soon as he got on the train. Let Garvey sulk.

Ferris got home late and found Fairfield deserted. Void of stars, the night sky was a matte screen braceleted by light pollution. A group of young women and *servero* Exfractians loitered around the water fountain outside the train station. Ferris waved, the Exfractians waved back, and rounded the corner to the apartment complexes.

A dreary silence hung in the air inside the apartment. Ferris left the Intercon paperwork on the kitchen bench and sunk into the couch. A message popped up on his corneal stream, anxiety and relief sparking up his spine. Not Garvey. Ferris settled back against the couch. It was Bishop, a long-time online friend, inviting him to play.

Ferris started the game and swiped a finger across his temple, projecting the title screen on the wall. Bishop's greeting blared across the room. Ferris quickly disconnected sound from the speakers to talk to Bishop over a private neural link.

'Hey, man, how you goin'?'

'I'm great, but you sound shitty,' Bishop chirped in his near-perfect New Jersey accent. 'Garvey still busting your balls?'

'When isn't he?'

'I don't know why you haven't kicked that *regio* brat to the curb.'

'Yeah ... I don't know either.'

'You okay? What happened?' Bishop's voice became gentler, caring.

Ferris took a deep breath and recounted the day. How the Intercon appointment struck a nerve and turned into an argument with Garvey about the dionide, and then some Exfractian construction workers went and added insult to injury. Bishop was quiet, taking in the information.

They swiped through the character carousel and chose their stage. A swirling blue corridor appeared on screen as their setting and characters loaded. Bishop released a tense breath over the link, it crackled with minute static.

'You know I'm always honest with you, man. Those construction workers are right, in a way.' Bishop's tone was careful. 'Garvey is *regio* and, naturally, will always remind you that you're *servero*. It's how he's been raised.'

'That's not an excuse,' Ferris countered.

'*I know,* Ferris, but you've gotta understand his reasoning if you want to fix the situation. You gonna hear me out?'

Ferris paused, bit his lip. 'Yeah, go for your life.'

'Garvey's grown up thinking our caste is his property. Yeah, maybe he's grown out of it a bit since being with you, but – what's that human saying – *old habits die hard*?' Bishop explained as his character stalked down an alleyway. 'Things won't change today, maybe they will a hundred years from now, but are you willing to stick around and help him out of his "habits" until then?'

Ferris chuckled and moved his character to a hiding place. 'I mean, you're right, I just ... I thought things would be different here.'

'It almost is, there's no caste system on Earth. We came here to get away from it, so why did he come here? The system has been crumbling for centuries on Exfracta, and the old *regio* hate that. Garvey didn't come here to be a new Earth citizen or whatever. He came here as an Exfractian that wants Earth to be the Exfracta from a million years ago.'

The apartment door beeped. Garvey was home.

'I've gotta go, I'll talk later.'

'He's back?'

'Yeah.'

'Alright, later then, be *civil*,' Bishop laughed.

Ferris disconnected their neural link and the game projection, putting his controller aside. Garvey turned on the lights. He didn't look at Ferris.

'Where've you been?' Ferris asked.

'Went to see my cousin,' Garvey answered and gestured to the wall. 'Don't stop playing on my account.'

Ferris stood up and approached the kitchen bench. 'No, we have to talk.'

'Oh,' Garvey finally looked at him. His mouth quirked down at the corners, but he seemed unperturbed. 'We're having *that* talk, are we?'

'Yeah ... I think so,' Ferris pursed his lips.

Garvey's face was flat, bored. 'This is about the dionide?'

'Not really.'

'It's the whole *regio-servero* thing, isn't it?'

Ferris shrugged. 'It's influenced most of the issues between us.'

Garvey nodded, gaze dropping to the floor. He clutched the kitchen bench. A long time coming, it seemed they'd both made their decisions before they saw one another.

'I don't suppose there's any way we can repair this?' Garvey asked.

'Do you want to fix this?'

'Do you?'

Garvey wanted to see Ferris' answer, to see if he'd keel over like he had done in the past. Ferris swallowed hard and shook his head.

'I think you and I came here – to Earth – for different reasons and got together for different reasons.'

'What do you mean?'

Ferris cleared his throat, feeling it grow tighter. 'When we met, I wasn't sure if going further was right because we're different castes. Still, I gave it a shot 'cause we're not *servero* and *regio* here. But over time, you leaned into our castes more and –'

'Get to the point,' Garvey snapped.

Ferris stuttered, taken aback. No chance of fixing it. Garvey had made his choice on where he stood: always in control, above Ferris.

'This lasted longer than expected, I think we've overstayed our welcome with one another. I left Exfracta to get away from the caste system, so I won't let you keep treating me like we're back home.'

'Ferris,' Garvey's tone was tired, worn, 'it's not the caste system, it's not just me "treating" you like a *servero*. You're impatient, you've got a temper, you haven't changed your attitude and –'

'And you thought the best way to deal with my attitude was to criticise me and – and control what I –'

Garvey rolled his eyes. 'I've never controlled –'

'You have! If I'm not speaking English, you won't talk to me in Exfractian, you hate hearing the *servero* –'

'Oh, I'm not being lectured by you,' Garvey hissed and trudged past Ferris. He called out from the hallway, 'I'll start packing my stuff and get out by Sunday.'

Ferris grit his teeth and clung to the bench. He would've cried out of frustration and disappointment if he had the function. He could hear cabinets slamming and clothes being shuffled around in the bedroom.

A stunted breath escaped through his teeth. There was no home for him on Exfracta, even with his own caste. Every home he had tried to build here collapsed with his efforts to make them stronger. Change, *harmony*, leapt further out of his grasp. For the first time in a long time, he was lost.

COLOURED RAINDROPS

Bethany Carter

A splinter of light breaks the darkness
eyes are closed; set on silver threads
like masses of tangled ribbons,
multiple rivers of thoughts
that flow fast and slow through foggy heads

Amid the roaring and tormenting crowds;
a swirl of colours, pale and bold
frustrations; weights of heavy mountains
making feelings of shame deeper and deeper
in response to anger – fierce and cold

Yet little beads, amid twisted thoughts,
are gems, raindrops, offering hope;
that differences, isolation and confusion
are accepted, appreciated; our salvation
in this world, we can cope

For oft we quiver in darkness alone,
Knowing not how to yearn for tomorrow
Lost in a tangle of complex memories
Waiting, watching for relief so near ...
and yet, the air hangs empty in sorrow.

FUN-SIZED DIVERSITY

Mohammad Awad

From
The *Jebel* of Lebnan,
Bankstown streets
Meet the
Depths of my Mother's womb,

From *Masjids*
To Kiki Ballrooms,

I had to learn
To Love
Where I was from.

To safekeep my dignity
while not fulfilling
The Angry Arab
Stereotype,
Project Western masculinity
To safeguard white fragility,

I mean it literally
When I say

You prefer us inanimate.

You want to be the Painters
of Our portraits,
To be seen with us
So we may exist
Within your frames,
Hanging as subjects
and cautionary tales
Of trusting White Men
to tell Our stories.

Only within
The palette of your brushstrokes
are we not distasteful,

You
are much like your cultural dishes;
You have no taste.

You prefer
Me

To my cousins.
Because
when I speak
I don't have the accent
or
At least not as much as
the rest of   them,
Not as rough
around the edges

Because

I trim my beard,
Don't wear my cultural gear
and when I teach you the proper way to say

Falafel

It falls on deaf ears.

Because of my lighter skin
Despite my ethnic origins
I'm easier to swallow.
To consume.

A walking, talking
Confetti of Culture
Pristinely packaged
to tell your friends you've managed
To catch another one,
Like I'm your fucking Pokémon.

Your
FUN-SIZED: Diversity Package.

Keep my Identity
in your pocket,
Pull it out
When it suits
You
Really don't understand what discrimination feels like.

How it tastes, bitter on your tongue
like biting on the forbidden apple,
much like Snow White's
evil Step-Mum
You
are the Problem,
disguising yourself as the Solution.
You truly do still desire to be the Fairest
of them all.

Even when you desire
Ethnic features,
they are only desirable on Ivory skin,
Shame brown women for their bodies
while you purchase an upgrade to thick-slim,
You have spent so long
Telling each other think-thin,
It is not our fault
The West has fallen
out of Love
with its kin.

Your children will not resemble you,
Your ancestors would not recognise you.

I know my children
will still have my nose,
will Awaken
and fall asleep
with the same set of curls,

my features are divine
and hereditary.
If my identity was a commodity
it would be the froyo flavour of the month,

Pick the skin tone
of your choosing,
Hair extensions
to match the season,
Your body only knows itself

in   fragments,
Take what you want.

Strip the persecution away
Mannequin papier-mâché
and contort the body into the shape
That pleases you,

that you so need to have.

Strip it of

The Language
            The Oppression
                        The Discrimination
                                    The History

Until all that is left
Are the Superficial symbols
That they represent;

But know that when you walk down these streets,
We can all see
that you're

hollow.

I'M SORRY

Zhipei Zheng

There are some things that I've been thinking about. Things that I can't get out of my head since you moved away. There are so many things I wanted to tell you, to ask you, but only after you left. Is it too late to go back in time and tell you how I really felt?

It was during the cool months of spring when you settled in our school. You looked different from the rest of us. Your features, skin colour, hair colour, eye colour and the shape of your face were all so different, that I couldn't help but sometimes wonder where you came from. A creature from a faraway land. You never talked. You couldn't talk even if you wanted to because you couldn't speak our language. You really weren't the same as us, were you?

There is something I've been thinking about these days. I treated you badly. I talked down to you, in front of you and behind your back. You never really understood what I was saying, so I continued. Whenever we played games of tag, you were always the one who was 'it'; the diseased animal that everyone was trying to run away from. Every time we played sport, you'd always be the last one to be picked, not because you're bad at sport, but simply because no one wanted you to be on their team. Eventually, everyone just got used to it. At recess and lunch, you'd always sit alone somewhere in the corner, either by yourself or with that other not-so-cool kid, eating food I'd never seen before. Sometimes you would offer to let me try some of your food, but I would always refuse. My food was better than yours.

Time passed quickly, and before we knew it, we were all taller, stronger, smarter and better at everything; except for you. You were always the same, except now you spoke and understood our language, but you never spoke often all the same. I remember one day when we were playing tag in the playground, and once again you were 'it'. We ran away from you, but you were faster than before, and somehow managed to tag me. I didn't like that, not in the slightest, I hated the fact that you were faster than me. I hated the fact that you were getting closer to me. I turned around and kicked you in the crotch. You screamed out in pain, but you never said a single word. It wasn't long before the teachers came and took you to the nurse's office and me to detention. After that day, every time I passed you, you would look away or down at the ground. At the start of the next semester, I never saw you again. You moved away.

I never thought much about anything back when I was young. However, as I've grown older, things have started to creep up on me like a ghost. I've realised how wrong I was. A sense of guilt and regret looms over me every time I reminisce about the past, each time growing stronger until it overpowers me to the point where I can't breathe. I should've treated you better and talked to you more. You always tried your best and there was so much good in your character. I should've known better. You and I could've been friends.

We could've been friends.

I should've realised earlier.

I'm sorry.

HINDI/ENGLISH INDIAN

Rhea L Nath

there is a language
that sits awkwardly on my tongue,
like food half-chewed.

twenty-one years I have lived in this country,
still I take a minute to read the signs:
'Saav-dhan, aa-ge an-dha mod hai'
'drive ... slow' this dumb mind translates.

my foot responds with the slow release of the accelerator,
perfectly mimicking my (slow) understanding
'krip-ya dhee-re chali-ye' I mouth, feeling utterly foreign.

on occasion, I curse my friends that smile
at the five-second delay for my tongue
to curl itself into the right angles.

‘*bhaiyya*’ becomes ‘bhaaya’ in my convoluted speech,
and men become women
when my vocabulary fails me.

twenty-one years I have lived in this country,
still I take a minute to thank the cleaners:
a rushed sentence, ‘see you soon’ and
‘do you understand me?’ in self-conscious tones,
utterly embarrassed of my awkward stutters.

each time, met with kind eyes
that somehow sympathise with this tongue
trapped in its privilege.

twenty-one years passed,
and English remains
my first language.

ENOUGH

Raz Badiyan

To those people I wish to be
I see them head to toe
They don't see me
This is my reality.

Their blonde hair
Green or blue eyes to match –
For what else is the colour brown,
But the substance of the ground.

Slender fingers type away
While mine are slow, round, tired
Behind the phone on which they write
Come summer, there's more to hide.

I am not mad at the opposites of me
Don't get this wrong, please.
Merely a reflection of thoughts
Of who I could superficially be.

HIGH COUNTRY

Scott Whittingham

Swirling thoughts gather momentum,
Of majesty, beauty and sweeping plains.
The highland's rugged ranges reveal,
An array of lichen, pigmy possums,
And intricate pale, yellow wildflowers.

An urge to gather a sample,
That is instantly self-denied.
Beyond the bounds of the law,
To cherish forever the uniqueness of adaptation.
Devoid of inevitable decline and dried keepsakes,
Remains absent from the notion of 'cabinet of curiosities'.

Cold, thinning air numbs the nose and ear,
Nearby, whistling gale and descending, an anguished, famished
crow.
The smell of distant patches of rain,
Waft as the head rises with deepened inhalation.

Hypnotically directed downwards,
Beyond rugged ridges and pale blue sky.

What beautiful creatures lay beyond the chilled shrubs?
Beyond the vastness of the descent through swirling, contrasting clouds.
The journey in this life will be rewarding when the simplest forms,
Are looked upon as an art form in their own right.
It is this engagement with ecosystems that encapsulates the soul,
Revealing a 'sense of place' that leads to an everlasting sensation.
There is a thirst for knowledge,
Within the complexities of places that affect other spaces.

Swirling thoughts gather momentum,
Of majesty, beauty and sweeping plains.
The highland's rugged ranges reveal,
An array of lichen, pigmy possum and pale yellow, wildflower.
The Australian landscape is vastly contrasting,
A country of extremes that supports life and rips it away.

THE LEAVES TURN BROWN IN SUMMER

Hannah Roux

It's spring and all the winter grass,
moist and crackling in my hands,
is bladed green, still half undead.
I lay my head on stems and leaves,
my tingling cheeks, my aching eyes
(blinking, open and afraid)
burnt to ash.
They're strong – the sun and the sky
that sting to look at.

It's spring and also winter still,
for every bud of green
a crumbling gum leaf drifts and falls,
red, yellow, brown or icy grey,
and splinters into all its parts –
dead crackle after summer's fire,
dies again on new spring's pyre.

Full fathom five your father lies,
and he has that fire in his eyes
by which the leaves were burnt,
the stones unleashed.
A coral fire – pink, white, and brown
turns red and grey and tumbles down
like dust-mote gums.
Scents of their death
spread with the new grass smell.

MOONLIGHT MOTEL

Ivy Waters

[Autumn, 2018]

The slowly dying sun glinted off stories of shining windows, glass broken and half gone. Grass and moss crawled over tumbled bricks, driven by moisture clinging to broken pipes and one long since stilled fountain. Behind these vestiges, the surviving structure soared up, low light turning it a warm golden pink. It had never looked this magnificent in its heyday. Or perhaps he had always been too distracted by what lay inside its walls, and by what lay outside, to notice. So many details of that time have been wiped from his mind, crumbled like the building itself. But he still remembered clearly the embrace of those walls and of the man within them.

[Winter, 1955]

Raphael burst, shivering, into the small lobby, the door slamming shut from the gust of wind at his back. He shrugged his arms out of his rough blue coat, letting it drape over his shoulders.

'Room 412?' he asked the man behind the counter, who nodded

and dialled before sticking the phone out to him, cord scraping against the plastic barrier.

'Hello.'

'Raphael, love,' came the reply, and he let himself melt ever so slightly, 'come on up.'

'Coming,' he sang, and handed the phone back to the man. He held it to his ear long enough to hear the click on the other end, signalling that it was safe to send the visitor up, then jerked his chin in the direction of the stairs before returning to his comic book. The Moonlight Motel picked its receptionists for one quality: indifference. They embodied it wonderfully. He nodded to the unseeing man and began the four-floor ascent.

[2018]

He ran his gaze along the broken windows, wondering whether he could identify the room. He thought he had found it, one from the corner with wild violets growing along its walls, but they all looked the same now. Hell, they'd looked the same back then too. If it hadn't been for the plain brass numbers on the doors, dulled from age but shined by hundreds of fingertips nervously smoothed over them across the years, you would never have been able to tell one room from another. Through the years, identical spaces had housed identical experiences, over and over. The history that lay in these walls was the shared history of countless people facing the same cages outside of them and finding the same freedom within.

[1955]

Adam opened the door, and Raphael nodded to him, doing his best to emanate what they both knew was an entirely false casualness. The corner of Adam's eyes crinkled as he half smiled back and extended a hand. Raphael took it as he shut the door behind them, their palms warm against each other. Suddenly, that one point of heat had spread, sending burning tendrils out to embrace his body a second before Adam did. Then his back was against the door, Adam's arms around him and his lips resting between his shoulder and neck. His coat hit the floor behind him, and he felt his back arch, separate from voluntary movement or consciousness. He let it for a moment, succumbing to the magnetic pull, before he wrapped his hands around the other man's hips, palms brushed by soft cotton covering smooth warmth, and lifted him away. Stepping forward, he pulled them both towards the bed, twisting them at the last moment. The mattress bounced beneath them as they landed, Adam's arms bracketing Raphael's chest. All of a sudden, they were both laughing, chests expanding with relief and desperation and freedom and something else entirely as Adam lowered himself and brought their lips together.

[2018]

It hadn't ever been officially branded as such – couldn't have been – and Raphael had sometimes wondered exactly how they dealt with the straight couples who had undoubtedly wandered across their bounds and who could have brought the institution crashing to its knees. But somehow it had survived – survived until it was no longer needed. He'd experienced an entire love within that building. He took a step closer and spread his palm across the crumbling wall. Infused with the warmth of the sun, it was reflected back into his aching fingers, decades of emotion sunk into bricks and embodied in heat, even as the sharp protrusions scraped his skin.

[1955]

Raphael leant out of the bed, coming perilously close to tipping over before he managed to grasp his coat off the floor and tilt back. The sudden shift in balance made him fall back onto Adam, who opened his eyes and laughed. Grinning, Raphael pulled a flask out of an inside pocket and threw the coat back across the room with an air of triumph. Uncapping it with one thumb, he took a sip before offering it to Adam.

'It's noon,' he pointed out, taking it anyway.

Raphael winked. 'Hasn't stopped you before.'

Shrugging, Adam raised it to his mouth, then lowered it again, barking out a laugh of surprise.

'This isn't Jacks.'

'I never said it was.'

He drank a mouthful, smile twisting the corners of his lips.

'And why did you put orange juice in a flask?'

Raphael shrugged. 'Didn't have a bottle spare.'

'I see. Didn't have anything to do with wanting to get me back for last month's noodle incident?'

'Oh, absolutely not,' Raphael replied, a twinkle in his eye. 'Me? Harbour a grudge against you for ruining my favourite shirt? Never.'

'That shirt deserved everything that was coming to it.'

'Well, despite your horrendous fashion opinions, I would obviously never set out to trick you.'

Adam shook his head, mimicking Raphael's mock innocence, then grinned and leant in, pressing cool orange-flavoured kisses to his lips as he pressed the flask back into his hand. 'Why the sudden desire for sobriety?' he asked as he leant back.

Raphael regarded him carefully, assessing the angle of his shoulders and the colour of his eyes, reading how deep his reply should go. A slight tilt of his head, and he made up his mind.

'I needed to see you. Clearly. It's been a long fortnight.'

A shadow passed across Adam's face, but before he could pursue it, he had rolled over and was straddling Raphael's hips with his face in the crook of his shoulder, teeth scraping sensitive skin. Raphael laughed and curled his fingers into the waves of hair at the nape of his neck, thoroughly distracted from whatever they had just been discussing.

[2018]

Despite everything, his strongest memories of this place, and of Adam, were still of laughter. Of his head thrown back and shoulders wide, of joy filling up a small room until it felt as if it would overflow. Its name notwithstanding, sunshine had filled that building inside and out, lighting up the dark corners they had lived in. Here, now, the light was fading, and the temperature was dropping, but within those walls, he had never been cold. Not really. Not in the way he was outside them, where the world did its best to threaten his very existence.

[1955]

The chill of the room was starting to creep into the warmth of the bed. Raphael reached down and pulled the thin sheet over them, huddling further under and closer to Adam beside him. He bent his head and brushed his lips across Raphael's curls, and he sighed. His heat was infectious and addictive, and Raphael curled still further into him, chest to chest, and kissed the wide curve of his shoulder. Here, on a too small and too thin mattress in a bare room was the only place he felt at home, the only place he ever truly felt safe. As they lay there, he could feel the tension seeping out of Adam as well, muscles softening under his hands. He reached down with one hand, grasping Adam's where it lay over his hipbone, and rolled onto his back. He shifted up so that he was resting on his chest, their fingers still intertwined, and tilted his head back to watch his face. He raised his fingers to his mouth, imitating a cigarette, not quite ready yet to break the silence with spoken words. A faint grimace passed across Adam's features, quick enough that Raphael would have missed it if he hadn't been watching him so closely. He shook his head.

'I'm quitting.'

Raphael frowned in question. Rather than explaining, though, Adam placed his free hand under Raphael's shoulders and urged him upward, capturing his lips in a breathless kiss as soon as he was close enough. The space between them seemed almost to compress by itself, and Raphael lifted a hand to Adam's chin, the sensation of his palm scraping across fine stubble sending shivers up his arm before he drew back. Adam looked at him with heavy eyes, grip so tight it was bordering on painful. Raphael raised his eyebrows gently, and the pressure on his skin eased ever so slightly.

'I love you,' Adam started, a sharp edge of heartbreak to the words.

[2018]

His funeral had been last week. Raphael had arrived, assuming he would sit in the back row, speaking to and recognised by no one. And he knew that would hurt, that an old awareness of an outsider status, with its dull blade, would be revived within him. But he had to go, couldn't miss this chance to acknowledge the man who'd meant – and in some way still did mean – so much to him.

He'd been prepared to be unseen. But instead a woman in her late forties with familiar peaked blonde hair and eyes red from crying, had wended her way across to him and tapped him on the shoulder.

'Excuse me. Are you Raphael?' she'd asked, and he'd been entirely unsure of the correct answer. There was no easy reason for him to have known Adam, other than the real one, and he had no wish to tarnish a dead man's image with a truth long vanished.

'Pa had this photo,' she continued, 'of him and a man he called Raphael, from when he was a lot younger. He told us about him, and you look ... a lot like him.'

'Yes,' he had replied, transported worlds away by the explanation. 'I'm Raphael ... what did he tell you?'

'That you were in love.'

[1955]

'I love you.'

'I know.' Raphael could hear the catch in Adam's voice. He smoothed a hand against his chest and waited. These silver linings were never divorced from their clouds.

'But I can't leave –'

He cut Adam off, 'I know.' He shut his eyes. It wasn't over yet.

'This has to be the last time.'

They'd promised this hundreds of times before, sworn that they couldn't and wouldn't see each other again, and every time it had been followed by simple codes in burnt letters and too brief but all too necessary meetings in a fourth-floor room. This was not a new set of words from Adam, but something felt different this time. The timbre of his voice was lower, rumbling through his chest in vibrations that Raphael could feel, that were causing his own body to shudder. His heart beat faster and stronger under Raphael's palm, as if something were trying to force it out of his body and into the other man's.

'What is it?' he asked softly, not wanting the answer but knowing he needed it.

'Louise ... she's pregnant. I'm going to be a father.'

Contradictory emotions clashed against each other – an unavoidable happiness for the man he loved, who he knew had wanted this as long as he'd been able to; a horrid deep-seated jealousy that his wife was going to get a part of Adam that he never could have; overwhelming tenderness at the image of Adam smiling down at a gurgling baby who had his eyes; and most of all a cavernous misery and loss, knowing that this was it. This was over. He couldn't risk putting his child in danger, unborn or no, and Raphael would never have asked him to.

'Her brother's a doctor,' was all he managed to say, fixating on the explanation to the statement which had urged Adam into speaking – that he was no longer smoking. 'The new studies on cigarettes ... '

He nodded. 'I can't do anything that could harm them.'

'I know.' Inside his head, that had been a tortured wail, but it came out low and soft and sad. He was not going to show him how much it hurt. He was not going to make it harder for him.

'I love you,' Adam repeated, voice breaking. He pressed the

heel of his hands into his eyes, tears leaking through regardless. Raphael broke with him, gathering him into his arms and burying his face against his shoulder.

'I love you.'

They stayed there, frozen in each other's arms, for what felt as if it were time immemorial, daring the world outside to freeze with them.

[2018]

His joints creaked and protested as he lowered himself onto one of the many boulders scattered behind the fading building. The folds of his coat settled around it, and he reached down, pulling out a rectangular whiskey bottle from a large pocket, the orange-hued contents conspicuously not those it had once contained. Unscrewing the cap with a firm grasp, he raised it to the crumbling building in front of him.

'To love,' he murmured, then poured a shot's worth onto the ground. He took a swig himself, swirling the acidic liquid around his mouth as he watched the liquid soak into the dirt, soil absorbing whatever nutrients it could. The sun finally dipped below the horizon, moon now clearly visible behind him, and he levered himself up. He took his time walking back around under the moonlight, despite the chill beginning to seep into his bones. When the car parked out front came into view, he stopped and leant one hand against the wall behind him, saying a final goodbye to the man he'd only ever see again in his daughter's eyes, and in an old black and white photo of the two of them laughing with their arms around each other. Something in him, something that had been disrupted long ago, settled deep into place, and he sighed.

The car's headlights came on, and he smiled. Walking over, he saw the man sitting in the driver's seat tighten the rainbow scarf that he still insisted was required driving attire, despite not having been in a convertible for nigh on two decades. After he had successfully manoeuvred himself into the passenger seat, he leant over and kissed him lightly.

'You okay, Raph?'

Raphael nodded. 'Yeah. I'm okay.'

'Alright.' He shifted gears and started backing out. 'Let's go home, then. I'm starving. We still have some of that casserole, so if you make salad, I'll do the bread and that should be enough for dinner ... '

The dinner-based monologue faded into a comforting background hum beside Raphael as he watched the Moonlight Motel disappear from sight. A silver glow suffused it now, as the full moon rose above it, and he smiled and rested his hand over his husband's, wedding bands aligning.

'I love you,' Raphael said as they turned a corner and the rear-view mirror showed nothing but open road.

He glanced over quickly, expression soft, before returning his gaze to the road in front of them.

'I love you too. So, casserole for dinner?'

'Casserole for dinner,' Raphael agreed.

I THINK OF CLOTHES IN PERSONAL LATIN

Misbah Ansari

How are you to define clothes,
Or keep calling them clothes?

When you build definitions for them on corduroy leaves,
Paint them white and green.

I walk on streets and think
Jacket holographia for a girl ensconced in a puffy coat
Like the sun that got bit by the caterpillar of holographs and now
Just glints through electrically dainty silvers, pinks, and blues.

I also think of *Piercing magicia* for the boy at the rally
His face full of piercings,
For he holds silver like a broken coronet and coils all the metal
Till his hands are exchanged for tangerines.

Oh, speaking of tangerines, I think of *Hijab chimeria*
In shops with hijabs of every neon,

As if the city opens just for her on a dark Wednesday afternoon.
She is the heroine in colour handling her coffee and shaved ice
As she bites into it.

I think of ice and remember *Feather etherelia*,
Cropped at the waist and spread across my bosom.
I fly and fly and rest until the feathers are streaked
With a tinge of brown.

Oh god, how much do I fall in love and create
Words for fabrics, metals, skin in varied countenances –
The moonlight casting different reflections of people
When wolves sing the ball music and all you do is
Howlingly stare.

PRESSURE

Sarah Carol Hughes

Over years and years
hands of the world
press, push, twist the young heart
into an invader.

Blackened and crumbling
in the chest, imprisoned
behind the ribs.

Until the pressure, denser than grief,
heavier than long-worn sorrow,
soundlessly shifts and shudders.

A flower smothered
between pages of a book.

A subtle release,
a change in Pressure,
reveals a diamond

forged inside the raw remnants
of a child's once-heart.

BURNING THE MASKS

Anastasia Taig

Dark suns are rising
as memories melt and disappear

I peel the pages from my skin
shedding a lifetime's worth,
scattering ashes in my wake.

There fall the cinders of compliance,
the shreds of meekness and of reservation,
the bloodied scraps of feminine reserve.

They burn, they die in me
and something Other rises

I drop the final page – the Virgin's veil
I taste the flames upon my tongue

I bear no mask.
I wear no face.
I am the fire.

FILTHY RICH

Harold Legaspi

They feed off the crusts I leave behind in boxes I consume daily. There are those who polish my shoes by craning their backs, on the verge of snapping. I pay them to listen to me talk because it feels good to be heard. I adore the sound of my own voice. I donate squillions at fundraisers and present my offering with a giant cheque – a brouhaha – the least humble of all. Nations have asked my chief execs for aid. I hand out squillions more so I can dominate the unequal playing field and exercise border control. My wealth will fund generations of my heirs. My heirs won't be ratty like theirs because I'll send mine to proper boarding schools, the kind J.K. Rowling tells us about in her books. I'll leave a legacy like Derek Zoolander when he opened THE ZOOLANDER CENTER FOR KIDS WHO CAN'T READ GOOD AND WHO WANNA LEARN HOW TO DO OTHER STUFF GOOD TOO! They'll worship my statues when I am martyred for telling it how it is: that money is God and God is money. That money can buy love. That money can buy an army to fight my battles. That money is ammunition. That money is *blood red,* not *green.* That money is heaven and hell and all the bits in between.

Aarhus Pride #1

Djuna Hallsworth

Aarhus Pride #2

Djuna Hallsworth

Aarhus Pride #3

Djuna Hallsworth

Colourism

Yasodara S. B. W. Puhule-Gamayalage

Genetic Diversity

Scott Whittingham

Oak Tree

Memi Adams

Pine Tree
Memi Adams

Beyond Religion and Diversity

Scott Whittingham

Banksia

Scott Whittingham

Elle Est L'univers 1

Keesha Field

Elle Est L'univers 3
Keesha Field

DINNER IN THE UNDERGROUND

Elizabeth Wheeler

Allow me to introduce myself, your nameless narrator. I am here only to offer personalised commentary on the odd dinner party that follows. But I heard that you wanted to know about this strange story, and so here I am to tell it and explain it. I'm sure it would be hard to comprehend without my genius additions to help you along the way ... can you feel my sarcastic wink? Because it's there. Anyway, let's begin at the start of the night.

Arthur's chair screeched against the stone floor when he pulled it out from under the table. He glanced around at the guests surrounding his table and offered a sheepish wave before he sat down. In an attempt to avoid following their host's example, the Ulris family tried their best to pull their chairs out without making a noise.

To understand this setting, you must understand a fundamental difference between Arthur Stilleno's family and his dinner guests, the Ulris family. The Stillenos are from the Catacombs of Priscilla in Rome, and the Ulrises are from Altamira, Spain. You see what I mean, right? Let's proceed.

Only once all the Ulrises were seated (meaning Mama

Ulris, Pa Ulris, Jericho Ulris and Lalla Ulris) along with Arthur Stilleno, did Arthur's wife come through the eastern tunnel from the kitchen. Following her was Arthur and Veranda's only child, Fontana Stilleno. Fontana had inherited her mother's beauty, being fair-skinned (as is natural for those who live in catacombs) with light auburn hair and gentle grey eyes. Her mother has much the same features but is quite the plump beauty. Arthur ... well, he's not much to look at. On a spectrum of beautiful to ugly, Arthur would land somewhere in the ambiguous middle.

Veranda and Fontana set the steaming dishes on the table. For every meal in the Stilleno's cave, they had a vegetable dish, meat, and grains. The vegetables were a mash of eggplant, spinach, tomato, and olives, with rosemary and dill and cumin; all things that were not meant to be combined but which Veranda did indeed combine. I'm sure if you had learnt how to cook from a skeleton in Rome's fourth-century catacombs, you would also combine things in such a way.

The meat was rather ordinary to contrast the unusual vegetables; just a platter of nicely cooked chicken laid alongside a few steaks to offer choice. The grains were the most unremarkable of all, a coloured multigrain rice of which Fontana scooped a good portion onto every plate before she finally sat down.

'Impressive spread, Veranda,' Pa Ulris nodded.

His words were a compliment to the cooking style, while his nod meant he was satisfied with the variety of food. The things his family ate back in Altamira could almost be described as the opposite to the spread before them. In Altamira, they preferred noodles over rice, milder vegetables with fewer herbs (although that was less a quality of Priscillian cooking than Veranda's own invention) and tended to eat duck or pork rather than beef or chicken. But to Pa Ulris, Veranda's cooking was not so extremely different from the food of Altamira. It still appeared mildly appetising to him, which is more than I could say for myself. And if you could smell it, you wouldn't want to eat it either, I'm sure.

And I wouldn't have been alone in thinking this. Jericho eyed the food with a subtle look of disdain on his face, lips curling down and eyebrows wrinkling inwards. Lalla Ulris didn't seem to be paying the food much attention at all. There was something – ahem, *someone* – more appealing to her at the table.

Needless to say, the full meaning of Pa Ulris' nod went beyond Veranda. She beamed and her pale cheeks illuminated with a pleasant pink blush.

'Anything for you, Pa Ulris. It's so rare that you make it to Priscilla, after all. Please, help yourselves to the food.' Her words were exactly what she meant, no gestures needed to elaborate, but still she gestured to the table. 'You'll have to tell me how the meat is, I'm a vegetarian myself so I can't vouch for the flavour.' Veranda added a chuckle. She rarely made any meat at all for her family, but a meal for guests would have been incomplete without it.

This time Pa Ulris' nod was in acknowledgement of something that he disapproved of. He'd heard about these new-wave eating habits and didn't think much of them for other people, but for someone he knew? Ridiculous. But his nod showed his resignation – he couldn't do anything about it.

The cavern descended into a cacophony of forks hitting plates. Everyone snatched up what they wanted before it had the chance to disappear down someone else's gullet. The meat was gone first. The rice made the vegetables better, but not good, so those were the last to go. Conversation was sparse until everyone had eaten enough to settle their growling stomachs.

'So, tell me about Altamira. We haven't had the chance to visit yet, but Arthur and I are always talking about it,' Veranda smiled at her husband, who quickly agreed. You'll find that Veranda and Arthur Stilleno are *always* in agreement.

'You are always welcome,' Mama Ulris reminded Veranda. 'Our caves are very beautiful, covered with ancient art and such.'

She found upon trying to speak that the words to describe the murals in the Altamira caves just wouldn't come to her. Her frustration was made visible by a quirk of her mouth, a tap of her finger. How could one explain in mortal words the paintings of immortal beings, the use of shadow and light in the cave drawings to express the struggle of the human soul at that time? There weren't words. And having been to Altamira myself, I will tell you, there really aren't any words.

'Our caves also have some ... artwork,' Arthur thought about it for a minute, about what to call the strange scenes from the Christian Bible that decorated the walls. Artwork, yes. He nailed it I must say. 'We'll take you around, to see them I mean, after dessert.'

Arthur tried a smile, but it really didn't work. Mama Ulris smiled back, her fingers tightening defensively around her fork.

'Of course, we'd love to see them. Who knows when we'll be back in Priscilla, right? Might as well see everything while we're here.'

Mama Ulris finished the last of her allotted rice and stood up from the table, forgetting momentarily the floor was stone and the chair legs were metal. The awful scream of the chair reverberated through everyone's eardrums and her son Jericho stared at his mother with dead eyes. She smiled to cover her embarrassment.

'Oh, right now? Well, alright,' Arthur wore his surprise plainly on his face as he carefully picked his chair up to step away from the table. He eyed his wife, who eyed him back, and they both stood ready to take the Ulris' around their caves.

'I'm not done eating!' Lalla Ulris squeaked. Her voice was small and delicate, like her figure. Her mother tapped Lalla's hands, at once telling her to shush, stop eating, and stand up.

Lalla looked at Fontana and caught her smile, then the two girls got up to follow their parents to the hall. Jericho sat at the table, mechanically eating as if he'd heard nothing of the artwork. He ignored Mama Ulris' glance, and she in turn ignored him. He was left at the table alone, the soft echo of his chomping the only remaining sound.

Arthur Stilleno led both families through a twisting hall into a larger cavern. He stopped with his chest puffed out in front of a wall decorated in shadowy maroon shapes.

'There it is, our pride and beauty,' he announced, lifting a hand in reverence for the painting.

Fontana and Veranda glanced at their guests in concern. They wouldn't say it aloud, but I know they were as embarrassed by Arthur's behaviour as I felt having only observed this encounter. You see, Arthur is simply a bumbling fool. But I'm sure he means well.

Papa Ulris stepped up closer to the wall and squinted at the red shapes as if that would make them clearer. Obviously, it didn't. Still, he nodded, and brushed a hand reverently across the stone wall beneath the shapes.

'What is it?' he asked.

Arthur huffed. 'What, you can't tell? It's the mother Mary from the Christian books. Isn't she just divine?'

Neither family practised much religion. I imagine it's hard to find a church in the catacombs. Ha.

It's fair to say that Arthur had no idea what he was talking about; he'd never read any such 'Christian books' and he barely knew the name of Mary. But such is the nature of the Stillenos that despite knowing nothing, they will still speak. And such is the nature of the Ulris' that despite knowing their hosts talked complete crap, they held their silence.

They stood looking at the cave painting a bit longer, Pa and

Mama Ulris both pretending that they cared about it enough to want to stare at it before they turned to head back to the dining room.

Their sudden turn caught their daughters by surprise, and Fontana and Lalla were caught holding hands.

Silence, like you've never heard before. Does that make sense? *I* think it does.

Lalla and Fontana were frozen, caught in an intimate act they never meant for their parents to see. Holding hands – oh dear, am I right? They all stood mildly frozen, a million thoughts running through each parent's head, as they debated what to say; even Arthur was thinking before speaking. But his wife couldn't help it and she belched the first sentence that came to mind.

'Thank God it's not Jericho!' She pulled a hand across her face in relief. Then, realising what she'd said, and thus having earned the attention of everyone there, she stuttered. 'You see, well. Arthur, you know right? I'm sure – I mean no harm, Mama Ulris, Pa Ulris, but Jericho ... There's just something a little not right about him.' She squeaked, as if making her voice softer could lighten the impact of her words.

It either worked, or Jericho's parents agreed enough to not care about the words. 'You are not wrong.' Mama Ulris sighed. She patted Lalla and Fontana's clenched hands as she walked past them, heading for the kitchen. Her husband followed, then her hosts, finally leaving the two lovers to follow. They exchanged blushing glances, both embarrassed and confused by what was a very strange encounter.

There were things to be done once they returned to the kitchen: dishes to be cleaned, the table to be polished, the floor to be swept, and anything else Veranda and Arthur could think of to keep themselves busy and away from the corner where the Ulris' were 'having a chat.' Arthur and Veranda didn't much mind who Fontana liked, as long as it wasn't Jericho, or anyone like him. On the other hand, it seemed to them that the Ulris family's discussion in the corner was rather heated.

'Lalla. You know how we feel about Priscillians.' Mama Ulris meanwhile, put a hand on her daughter's elbow. 'Never mind that Fontana is a sweet girl, we just feel ... ' She shrugged, sighed, and nudged her husband.

'We feel ... that you should have told us earlier.' Even if he was talking to his daughter, his eyes were on his wife for approval. She shook her head at him and tightened her grip on Lalla's elbow. 'We just want you to be careful of how close you get to Priscillians.'

Lalla smiled her angelic smile in a way that reassured her parents, and yet also promised absolutely nothing. Behind her, the Stilleno's ran out of things to clean in the kitchen and switched to chatting among themselves. Jericho sat alone at the table, looking rather forlorn without any food to mechanically chew. And me? I floated away from the Catacombs of Priscilla to come and tell this strange story to you, dear readers.

AS FIRE TO SNOW

Rosie Mulray

Across the foam and rolling sea
I stand alone and watch her ship
atop the cliff face. Howling gales
chill my heart and cruelly whip
my hair out to the ocean pale,
it pulls my love away from me.

I know that she is strong and brave,
a fury courses through her deep
she'll chase her glory 'cross the sea,
to take the skulls of foes to keep
as warnings dire, filled with mead.
Her spirit's ravenous and free,
the wind her guide and fate her steed.

And love, she loves as fire to snow
her heat fast melts the wintr'y cloak
that falls upon my shoulders two,
she breaks me down to ash and smoke,

each time we touch I love anew
I am undone before her glow.

So selfish I to keep her here
when well I know she must away,
perhaps a tincture, herb or brew
could make her change her mind, to stay,
forsake her bounty, shield and crew
then naught would I have left to fear;

But naught as well my love would be!
I cannot tame a fire so bold
and love what once was scorching hot,
then by my hand, reduced and cold.
My head knows what my heart does not,
I have to let her hie to sea.

What reason have we taken paths
so shadowed, treacherous and sheer,
each joyful moment with her tainted;
kiss and gesture laced with fear.
Entwined, we're singed and consecrated,
parted, cold as barren hearths.

Then let her go and break, oh heart,
in doing what we know is right.

Noble strength builds in my chest,
and though I want with all my might
to hold her tightly to my breast;
A burning kiss, and then we part.

And so, I stand and watch her ship,
with fractured heart and cold desire.
Wind that pulls at hem and hip
bears too my broken, brittle vow.
My fragile will consumed by fire,
I want her back to hold me now.

From high atop the cliff face then,
I'll look to the horizon true
each day 'till she returns to me;
my love lost in the churning blue.
The wind took her beyond my ken.

I look to sea and know not if
I'll see my love alive again.

MOTHER EARTH

Scott Whittingham

Earth Mother is united with all,
Creatures great and small.
The divine Mother looks over,
The mountains that are our bosom

With thirst we must suckle from grey sky.

Trickling through hands
They shall sprout above barren land
From deep within dark, nurturing richness,
Lay seeds that wait for the ideal moment.

We wait with emotional and physical constraints.
For that moment when thirst is quenched and hunger, satisfied
Some choose to lay dormant
When conditions are plentiful.

Australian seedpods are opened in extreme temperatures
New life arises from trees that have suffered the wrath of fire

Through eons of evolution they have learnt
The art of resilience and adaptation.

Each species of plant life unique,
Overcame their harsh environments
So must we overcome the hurt in our past.

Our wounds must be healed
Though there will always be scarring deep within
Like that of a felled tree.
The rings of distress and agony shall remain.

Only when we let the turmoil settle,
Will richness be gently accepted.

Fossils may be uncovered,
Brushed ever so delicately,
Analysed from all perspectives,
For a previous existence.

Would you rather have a bone?
Or the fresh fruits of life?

Let the skin be discarded,
To reveal delightful rewards.

DIVERSITY AND GENDER IN THE COMPOSITIONAL RELATIONSHIP OF ROBERT AND CLARA SCHUMANN

Katarina Grobler

Of the many well-known 'power-couples' to have graced the Western music canon, Robert and Clara Schumann's influential partnership remains one of the most beloved in Romantic literature today. Their success as individual artists can be attributed to a co-dependency formed early on in their careers. Their connection, which involved the exchange of musical themes, began in 1830, when Robert Schumann began to study under Friedrich Wieck, Clara's father. It continued well into their marriage, with Clara premiering her husband's works in the concert hall, elevating her reputation as a concert pianist and earning her a high status among prominent social circles of the time.[1] However, while much biographical content exists on the personal nature of their relationship, few scholars have focused solely on their compositional partnership. For example, early twentieth-century writers such as John N. Burke have stated that

1 Reich 2001.

Robert was 'an artist for eternity',[2] while Clara was 'a concert-giver for the moment.'[3] Although Clara is recognised foremost as a performer, her compositional output is more than substantial enough to research and draw comparisons between the two individuals as 'composers'.

While Robert Schumann's compositional output has been discussed at length, scholarship that explores Clara Schumann's compositions from an analytical standpoint is still lacking.[4] This can be partly due to the fact that many of her scores and manuscripts are missing or incomplete.[5] In addition, Clara frequently described herself as lacking in compositional talent, which she often attributed to her status as a woman.[6] Reasons for why she gave up composing after her husband's death in 1856 are complex, however it is assumed to be due to her increased responsibility as a single mother and the need to return to the concert stage as the sole financial provider.[7] Due to these reasons, research into her compositional work may have been

2 Burke 1940.

3 Fonseca-Wollheim 2019.

4 Only two recent comprehensive biographies exist: Reich (2001) and Klassen (2009). While they both show immense insight into all aspects of her life, neither provide an analytical focus on her creative work. Additionally, both are influenced and based on Berthold Litzmann's *Clara Schumann: Ein Kundstlerleben nach Tagebüchern und Briefen* (1902) which predominantly gives insight into Clara's personal relationships.

5 Reich 2001, 289.

6 Reich 2001, 216.

7 Reich 2001, 211.

neglected to focus on her influence in developing nineteenth-century performance practice. Additionally, issues of gender have inspired a different research angle: as a successful career woman and single mother, Clara has since become an ideal 'feminist' model of the nineteenth-century woman.[8] While such portrayals are fascinating and necessary, they again encourage a focus on her personal life rather than her creative work.

Throughout this essay, I will attempt to address this gap in the current discourse through an exploration of compositional diversity in Robert and Clara Schumann's works. Similarities will also be explored; in particular the motivic ideas, musical symbolism and personal influence shared between the two composers during their creative period. In a short essay, a comprehensive comparative analysis is not possible. Instead, I will explore some indicative trends and point the way for future work on the topic.

Aesthetic Differences

Although both composing at the height of the Romantic period, Clara and Robert Schumann had vastly different aesthetic views that they communicated through their compositions. While

8 Undoubtedly, Clara Schumann's accomplishments were monumental for a woman of her time. However, we cannot call her a 'feminist' in the contemporary understanding of the term; letters and diary entries in Reich (2001) reveal her complete compliance with the social roles and attitudes expected of women during the nineteenth century. Her motives were always driven by artistic goals, not by actions actively intended to further women's rights.

Clara became an ambassador for the virtuoso tradition and stylistic forms of the Romantic period, Robert Schumann pushed boundaries through cryptic symbolism and poetic expression.

We can already observe this difference from the earliest compositions of both Clara and Robert Schumann. Stephan Smith states that from Op. 1 *Abegg variations* – in which the theme spells out the name of Meta Abegg, Schumann's fictitious friend – Schumann began a life-long journey of exploring 'what's in a name' in musical terms.[9] At times, word symbolism is obvious, such as Abegg with its use of 'musical' letters as symbols, and at other times less so, with themes enclosed within ciphers.[10] With the creation of a fixed letter grid (Example 1), each word or name would follow a particular melodic shape. The use of this specific grid and word symbolism can be found in Robert's Op. 2 *Papillons*, Op. 4 *Intermezzos*, Op. 7 *Toccata*, Op. 9 *Carnival*, and in many of his later works, such as Op. 60 *Six Fugues on Bach* and Op. 68 *Album for the Young*. While other composers had used melodic codes in the past, Schumann's development in this area created a new level of connection between music and language in nineteenth-century writing. After falling in love with Clara, Schumann allegedly changed the top letter grid to D-H-A-B-C-E-F-G, also symbolically aligning Clara's initials with those of Schumann's two alter egos, Eusebius and Florestan.[11]

9 Smith 1994, 10.

10 Smith 1994, 10.

11 Smith 1994, 10.

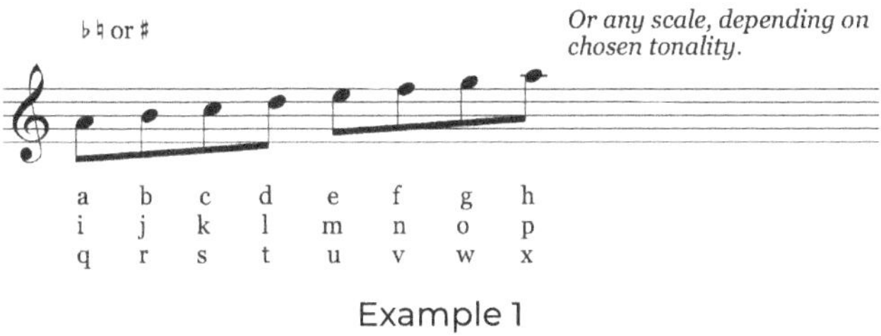

Example 1

Schumann's early compositional period (1830–1839) also features some directional tonal works. As defined by Wadsworth, these are works which begin and end in different (but unambiguous) keys, thereby suggesting hierarchal equality through associating keys ('dual tonality').[12] For example, in his Op. 4, No. 5 *Intermezzo*, Schumann moves from F major to D minor, as both compete for dominance throughout the piece. This has frequently been associated as representing Schumann's internal struggle between his two alter egos.[13] Additionally, Schumann's use of directional tonality, particularly in works such as the 'Florestan' movement from *Carnival*, allows him to create drastic contrasts between moods and emotional states. It is clear that from the start, Schumann's complex harmonic understanding and use of word symbolism gave him more freedom to manipulate the concept of structure in his works. Although he worked within the parameters of the Romantic tradition, he advanced the style in a unique way.

12 Wadsworth 2012, 1.

13 Wadsworth 2012, 2.

In contrast, Clara Schumann's compositions reflect a strong obedience to the established clichés of nineteenth-century Romantic writing. Despite her talent for composition, she did not actively push boundaries, and instead preferred to become an advocate of the virtuoso tradition and brilliant style that characterised this period. We can assume this to be for a number of reasons – firstly, the greater part of Clara's compositions were written during her youth, when she followed instruction from her father and teacher, Friedrich Wieck. As per nineteenth-century tradition, the successful performing concert artist was both an interpreter and creator of music. Under her father's instruction, Clara's childhood compositions were designed to be performed at her own concerts and show off her technical prowess.[14] In essence: Clara composed because she *had* to, not necessarily because she was inspired to.

From her diary entries, we also know that Clara suffered from intense feelings of self-doubt about her compositional skills

14 Some speculation remains over whether these were Clara's own compositions or her father's. He took charge of every aspect of Clara's life, including her personal diary. Examples of some entries include: 'This month I composed a great deal, finished – among other things ... the first solo of a large Concert Rondo' (July 1833) and 'I completed the orchestration of my Waltzes on the 25th and wrote it out myself. Herr Meyer looked over the score.' (1835). However, evidence shows that Wieck's compositions vastly differed from Clara's style, and his frequent joyous expressions at the talent of her creativity assert that her compositions were indeed her own.

(especially so in later years).[15] These did not stem from a lack of education; Clara had attended formal harmony, orchestration, score-reading, and counterpoint lessons from the age of ten, and, under her father's strict regime, every single musical event in Leipzig from the age of six (including performances at the opera).[16] With such a strong formal education, we can assume Clara had a plethora of knowledge to access for creative writing – had she the desire. Occasionally she expressed the wish to compose, but after the resumption of her performing career, she largely avoided playing her own works in public, preferring instead to showcase the works of her husband.[17]

Evidence also shows that each of Clara's concert programs between 1833 and 1838 included an original composition.[18] Sadly, many of these scores have either been destroyed or lost, but according to Reich, they were crowd pleasers that likely reflected the popular style, similar to the compositions of Henri Herz, Johann Peter Pixis and Friedrich Kalkbrenner.[19] Among the first of Clara's works to be published include her Op. 1 *Quatre Polonaises*, Op. 2 *Caprices en Forme de Valse* and Op. 3 *Romance Variee.* Commenting on the *Quatre Polonaises*, a reviewer in Berlin's music journal *Iris* stated:

15 See heading 'Gender and Fugue' for further reference.

16 Reich 2001, 22.

17 Reich 2001, 216.

18 Reich 2001, 212.

19 Reich 2001, 212.

> What reasonable person wants to have school exercises printed, even if they turn out well? But that is the sorry fate of our time – not to take heed of art of the needs of the public, but only to pay allegiance to the purse or homage to vanity.[20]

Opinions from others were more encouraging – upon playing the third polonaise for Nicolai Paganini, the composer praised the young artist for her 'great feeling'.[21] While on a concert tour in 1847, a Prague newspaper even described her as a member of the 'new romantic school', associating her with contemporaries such as Chopin and Mendelssohn.[22] As Reich asserts, this 'romantic' style can be seen through features such as the bravura technique, lyricism and the 'singing' style, experimentation with popular forms like mazurkas, waltzes, polonaises, theme and variations, and even aesthetic ideals of fantasia and the supernatural (for example, her Op. 5 *Le sabbat/Hexentanz*) which we now identify as a key topic area in music from the Romantic era.

However, one work that is worthy of mention here is Clara's Op. 7 *Piano Concerto in A Minor* which was perhaps the most adventurous step Clara took out of the established Romantic tradition. Unlike the traditional concerto form, it is a single-movement work, including only a cello and piano duet in the

20 Reich 2001, 221.

21 Reich 2001, 290.

22 Reich 2001, 211.

Romanze section. Additionally, there is limited orchestral exposition before the entrance of the soloist in the opening of the piece, and the work contains no cadenza. Moreover, the harmonic structure is quite unconventional; the piece moves from A minor towards a coda that functions as a transition into A-flat major for the *Romanze*, and then back to A minor for the finale. Although not an abrupt change, one critic has likened this to 'the moods of women'.[23]

Interestingly, Clara asked Robert Schumann to help orchestrate the finale,[24] which follows more traditional interjections between the tutti and solo parts. Up until this point, Clara had only written miniatures, and while her solo writing was outstanding, her skills in orchestration were still developing. This is evident when we compare her orchestration of the first two movements, in which the orchestra merely accompanies the soloist, to the last, where there is much more textural interest and melodic interplay between the tutti and solo part. Nevertheless, the concerto did have a lasting influence on many contemporaries of the time – Robert Schumann's only piano concerto is also written in A minor, in which its middle section in the first movement also moves to A-flat major. Additionally, Brahms' second piano concerto also features a cello-piano duet in its *Andante* movement.

---

23 Reich 2001, 228.

24 Clara asked Robert to orchestrate the third movement in 1833, and the concerto was given its premiere in Leipzig in 1835 under the direction of Felix Mendelssohn. After several more performances and revisions, the full concerto was published in 1837.

Although both composers were dependant on each other during their early years of composition (e.g. from Clara's teenage years, Robert already depended on her to perform his works due to his hand injuries),[25] their creative direction was vastly different, despite their virtually identical context. Gender also plays a role here, especially as their careers developed. As a respected man, established writer, and German composer, Robert Schumann had more liberty in exploring unconventional ideas within his music. As a woman, Clara may have felt that this would be too big of a risk to take for fear of being harshly criticised, as it was already difficult to have artistic views validated by other men as a woman composing at the time. However, despite not living up to the nineteenth-century standard of the idealised 'progressive' artist, Clara's allegiance to the Romantic tradition meant that she became a master of its styles and forms.

Themes of the Beloved

Part of Robert Schumann's aesthetic also rested on the notion that music 'transcends its causal influences, but bears their imprint in character'.[26] However, the true influence behind his greatest works can be narrowed down very specifically to one main subject: Clara. In his 1994 essay, Stephen Smith writes:

25 Reich 2001, 212.

26 Smith 1994, 3.

Robert Schumann, Sonata in F Minor, op. 14, third movement, "Quasi Variazioni. Andantino de Clara Wieck."

Robert Schumann, Sonata in F Minor, op. 14, first movement, Allegro.

Example 2

In a letter of 1838, Schumann said, 'My Clara will know how to find the real meaning of [the *Davidsbundlertanze]* for they are dedicated to her in quite a special sense.' In another letter to Clara, regarding *Kreisleriana*, we find: 'You and one of your ideas are the principal subject.' The Op. 17 *Fantasie,* he told his betrothed, is 'one long wail over you.' And in 1837 he went so far as to say, 'I have but one thought to depict everywhere in letters and chords – Clara.'[27]

The 'Clara Theme' and its exact origin has been debated among scholars. One depiction is thought to be the notes C-B-A-G-Sharp-A[28] (Example 1), while other musicologists claim it to be a descending five note pattern starting on the third

27 Smith 1994, 6

28 Smith 1994, 6

degree of the scale, originating from the slow third movement of Schumann's Op. 14 *Sonata in F Minor*, 'Andantino de Clara Wieck' (Example 2).[29] Another possible source is Clara's Op. 4 '*Valses Romantiques*', in which the latter pattern becomes the main motif. Smith theorises that perhaps it was not a specific piece that inspired the theme but was one that became associated with Clara due to her frequent use of it.

Amusingly, in comparison, Clara never explicitly acknowledges Robert as inspiration for her works, except in her Op. 20 *Variations on a Theme of Robert Schumann*. However, there are many instances where Clara does reframe some of Robert's harmonic and motivic ideas.

For example, in the *Valses Romantiques*, bars 7–10 very closely resemble the 'Valse Allemand' from Schumann's *Carnival* (Example 3).[30] Similarly, she reframes a theme from one of Robert's 'Impromptus' in her Op. 3 *Romance Variee*, which she uses again to represent the composer in *Variations* (Example 4).[31]

Composed at the end of her creative period, her Op. 20 *Variations on a Theme of Robert Schumann*, is seen to be one of

29 Reich 2001, 220.

30 Reich 2001, 221.

31 Robert Schumann first identified this theme as Clara's own, as his 'Impromptus sur une romance de Clara Wieck' (composed in 1833) were based on the theme in Clara's Romance (composed 1831). However, scholars have traced back the theme to a diary entry from Schumann back in 1830, revealing that it was his conception.

Clara Wieck, *Valses romantique,* op. 4, measures 7-10.

Robert Schumann, *Carnaval*, op. 9, "Valse allemand," measures 9-12.

Example 3

Clara Wieck, *Romance variée,* op. 3, "Romanza."

Clara Schumann, Variations on a Theme by Robert Schumann, op. 20, Coda. measures 9-10.

Example 4

her more structured and formal works. The theme is explored in canon, recast in a major mode and in a chorale style.[32] According to Smith, it also showcases some of Clara's distinct compositional features: semitone dissonance, octave chromaticism and repeated use of appoggiaturas that pervade many of her works.[33] Commenting on the *Variations*, Joan Chissel states that it betrays Clara's 'allegiance to the decorative virtuoso tradition,'[34] and in his recording notes, James Sykes asserts that it is 'an exploration of piano colouration, resonance, and volubility.'[35] Dedicated to Robert as a birthday gift, it was the last composition he received from Clara before he was admitted to the mental asylum in Endenich. At this point in time, Johannes Brahms had begun spending more time with the Schumann's, and he sent his own work, Op. 9 (also titled *Variations on a theme of Robert Schumann*) as a dedication to Clara. In the final variation, Brahms also interlocks the two themes, paying homage to Clara's work (Example 5). As requested by Brahms, the two compositions were published as a pair by Brietkopf & Hartel in 1854.[36]

Gender and Fugue

It is interesting to note that the three male figures seen to be most significant in Clara Schumann's life: her father, Robert Schumann

32 Reich 2001, 233.
33 Smith 1994, 31.
34 Chisell 1983 in Smith 1994, 34.
35 Sykes in Smith 1994, 35.
36 Smith 1994, 31.

Variations on a Theme by Robert Schumann, op. 20, Coda. measures 9-10.

Johannes Brahms, Variations on a Theme by Robert Schumann, Variation 10. measures 30-32.

Example 5

and Johannes Brahms, highly valued her compositional skills and often encouraged her to write and publish more than she did.[37] Despite this, Clara's diary entries reveal severe self-doubt in her creative ability:

---

37 Previously tied to the responsibility of composing for her father, Clara now had requests to fill for her husband, Robert: 'Clarchen, do you perhaps have something for my supplement ... do compose a song!' and then in 1840; 'Write to me again of what you see and hear ... try to compose a song; you'll see how well it will turn out'. Despite this encouragement, Clara remained resistant in composing new works.

> I once believed that I had creative talent, but I have given up this idea; a woman must not wish to compose – there never was one able to do it. Am I intended to be the one? It would be arrogant to believe that. That was something with which only my father tempted me in the former days. But I soon gave up believing this. May Robert always create; that must always make me happy.[38]

In 1845, both composers undertook studies in fugue and counterpoint, which are reflected in their compositions at the time – for example, Robert Schumann's Op. 60 *Sechs Fugen* for organ, and Clara's Op. 16 *Drei Praeludien und Fugen* for piano.

Her studies during these years also influenced her Op. 17 *Trio in G Minor*, which showcases a fugato in the final movement. After its completion, she wrote in her diary: 'There is really no greater pleasure than having composed something and then to hear it' but later reflected that it was 'women's work, which always lacks force and occasionally invention.'[39] Despite this self-criticism, the *Trio* received great praise from critics and contemporaries. In 1860, her colleague, violinist Joseph Joachim, wrote, 'I recollect a fugato in the last movement and remember that Mendelssohn once had a big laugh because I would not believe that a woman could have composed something so sound

38 Reich 2001, 216.

39 Reich 2001, 216.

and serious.'[40] Evidently, social expectations which perpetuated a view that female composers could not exhibit the 'genius' quality of the great male composers such as Beethoven, Bach and Mozart, clearly affected the way in which Clara Schumann's compositions were received. Generally, Clara's works were prized for their innovative qualities against the measure of what a 'woman' could compose, rather than the artistry of the entire musical current of the time.

Undoubtedly, these gendered reviews had an effect on Clara's self-perception as a composer. During her study, she expressed statements such as: 'I cannot thank Robert enough for his patience with me,' and wrote to him: 'I have a peculiar fear of showing you my compositions; I am always ashamed.'[41] Evidently, she perceived Robert as the better composer in their relationship, and believed she could not live up to his creative expectations of her. This, however, was a false assumption – in their 1843 marriage diary, Robert shares his views:

> Clara has written a number of small pieces that show a musical and tender invention that she has never attained before. But to have children and a husband who is always living in the realms of imagination do not go together with composing. She cannot work at it regularly and I am often disturbed to think how many profound ideas are lost because

40 Reich 2001, 216.

41 Reich 2001, 216.

> she cannot work them out. But Clara herself knows her main occupation is as a mother and I believe she is happy in the circumstances and would not want them changed.[42]

Alongside her creative insecurity and this entrenched gender norm of the nineteenth-century wife subscribing herself fully to the domestic role, it is no surprise that Clara's compositional output became limited after her marriage to Robert Schumann.

Collaborative Works

A special composition in the repertoire of both composers is the Rückert Lieder, Op. 37/12. Published in 1841 with Robert and Clara's respective opus numbers, this work is a joint song cycle of twelve pieces based upon poems from Friedrich Rückert's *Liebesfrühling*. Under Robert Schumann's request, the song cycle was sent to editors and published without reference to the author of each individual piece in order to unite the two composers as 'one heart and one soul.'[43] However, from Robert's own copies we know that three of the songs (*Er ist gekommen in Sturm und Regen*, *Liebst du um Schönheit*, and *Warum willst du and're fragen*) were written by Clara, which she gifted to Robert as a Christmas present in the early stages of the collaboration process. With it came the inscription: 'Composed and dedicated to her ardently beloved Robert with the deepest modesty from

42 Reich 2001, 215.

43 Reich 2001, 238.

his Clara on Christmas 1840.'[44] As we can see, Clara again reveals her insecurities. Rather than a collaboration in the traditional sense, Clara's work here was more of a contribution to a composition, essentially written (and published without further notice) by Robert Schumann. Clara received the first copy of the joint cycle on her birthday in 1841, for which she expresses her embarrassment: 'Robert surprised me with the published Rückert Lieder, among them several of my own weak products.'[45]

Stylistically, the songs are very similar (an intentional decision to provide unity), and it is in this work where we can first truly say that the aesthetic ideals of both composers blend completely and are difficult to separate. Some of the features uniting the work include closely related keys (half are in A-flat and the rest in familial keys of a minor fifth or third below), as well as shared motivic material between the pieces.[46] For example, in Clara's *Liebst du um Schonheit* and Robert's *O Rose, Meer und Sonne*, both pieces begin with arpeggiation followed by a cycle of fifths progression, broken at the cadence (in both pieces – see Example 6).[47] This shows that while they worked independently on the pieces, Clara intentionally composed with some of Robert's completed works in mind. Unique for the time of its publication, this is the only work of true collaboration between the two composers.

44 Reich 2001, 238.

45 Reich 2001, 238.

46 Hallmark 1990, 16.

47 Hallmark 1990, 16.

a. Song 9, mm. 1–6, 15–18 (23–26).
1(2)
3
Ro - se, Meer und Som - ne sind ein Bild der
15(23)
Lieb - ste mein leigt ver - eint be - schlos - sen in dem Kelch der Ro - se nur.
(um her - vor - zu - brin - gen im Ver - ein der Ro - se Bild.)
b. Song 4, mm. 1–10, 15–18.
1(2)
3
Leibst du um Schön-heit, o nicht mich
lie - be! Lie - be die Son - ne, sie trägt ein gold' - nes
Haar!
15
Lie - be den Früh - ling der jung ist je - des Jahr!

Example 6

Conclusion

In essence, we can assert that the compositional relationship between Clara and Robert Schumann remained very complex throughout their life and partnership. While Robert's aims were to evolve traditional nineteenth-century music, Clara focused on exemplifying the clichés of this tradition in her own works. Even though they shared motivic materials and were inspired through each other's musical themes, their published works are vastly different in style, aesthetic, and form. This was also due to their different roles in that of the 'performer', in the case of Clara Schumann, and 'composer', in the case of Robert. Robert devoted his career to composition while Clara focused on her career as a concert artist and had limited opportunity to develop her compositional style (had she the desire to do so). As I have demonstrated, gendered views on the notions surrounding the quality of work able to be produced by female composers played a large part in discouraging Clara's compositional output. Anything less than satisfactory was quickly denounced as 'women's work' – simple, uncreative and intellectually lacking. Despite the support from her friends, family and spouse, Clara remained insecure about her creative abilities and continued to apologise (particularly to her husband) for her perceived inadequacies. Moreover, while I have outlined basic compositional links between the two composers in this essay, further research and work needs to be done in the musicological sphere to establish the value of

Clara's compositional output. Not only would this allow further insights into the musical relationship between the two composers, but also provide a balance to their often romanticised personal relationship. Nevertheless, as we have seen, their success was always interconnected; it is precisely because of this relationship that both composers were able to produce some of the most influential works of nineteenth-century repertoire.

References

Burke, John N (1940). *Clara Schumann: a romantic biography*. New York: Random House.

Chisell, Joan (1983). *Clara Schumann, a dedicated spirit: a study of her life and work*. New York: Taplinger Publishing Co.

Fonseca-Wollheim, Corinna (2019). Nancy B. Reich, scholarly champion of Clara Schumann, dies at 94. *The New York Times*, 11 February. https://www.nytimes.com/2019/02/11/obituaries/nancy-b-reich-dead.html.

Hallmark, Rufus (1990). The Rückert Lieder of Robert and Clara Schumann. *Nineteenth-Century Music* 14(1): 3–30.

Klassen, Janina (2009). *Clara Schumann: Musik und Öffentlichkeit*. Austria: Böhlau.

Reich, Nancy B (2001). *Clara Schumann: the artist and the woman*. London: Cornell University Press.

Smith, Stephan James (1994). Eloquence, reference and significance in Clara Schumann's Opus 20 and Johannes

Brahms' Opus 9. Ph.D. dissertation, University of British Colombia, Vancouver, Canada.

Wadsworth, Benjamin (2012). Directional tonality in Schumann's early works. *Music Theory Online* 18(4). http://www.mtosmt.org/issues/mto.12.18.4/mto.12.18.4.wadsworth.php.

THE MULTI-COLOURED ROAD TO AUSTRALIA

Vrishali Jain

Two years ago, I was diagnosed with a severe case of Polycystic Ovarian Syndrome (PCOS). The doctor also suspected that I was suffering from endometriosis.

I had my dream job; a job that afforded me the ultimate opportunity to write, read, write and read some more, but I was told that I had to make adjustments to my daily schedule, that I had to make my health, not my dreams or my ambition, a priority.

But you see, that is the case with youth.

We absolutely do what we want.

I was working in Delhi at the time. My job was on the line, a job that I valued above everything. A job that I was told time and again people of my age could only dream of. A demanding job that devoured me and that I wanted to devour me. For me that was the only way to succeed, absolutely nothing was more important than my dreams.

I made some changes, but I still wasn't making my health and my body a priority.

My PCOS worsened.

My menstrual cycles suffered, and I suffered right along with them. I had started bleeding clots and the pain was horrible enough to keep me tied to the bed for days at a stretch.

What was worse were the cramps. They'd begin suddenly and would have me doubling over in a moment. It was like a punch to the gut, only not with a fist, but with a brick.

I remember it as clear as day. It was a warm May afternoon and I had the latest ultrasound scans in my hand. The report read, '20–23 cysts or cyst-like formations detected in left ovary. 24–26 cysts or cyst-like formations detected in right ovary'.

Essentially, I was carrying around a total of forty-six cysts in my ovaries. Cysts that were enough to ruin my body in a way that would be very difficult to recuperate from. Already, my weight had gone beyond management and my hormones had their own sweet song that they danced to every month.

I weighed ninety-five kilos, I was unable to walk, and I was in horrible pain for the better part of every month.

I was all of twenty-four.

At this point you'd think I would've taken some time off, but I still continued to work. I think that was the only thing that kept me going.

To say my family was worried would be an understatement. At the time, I was living near my aunt, Bina *Bua* (*bua* in Hindi means paternal aunt). Lord bless her heart, she was the support that kept me standing upright. She would tend to me like a mum and hear me out like a friend. We shared a common love of books and she would talk to me about them for hours at a stretch. I would lie in her bed, and she would calmly feed me turmeric lattes to ease my pain.

She was also my father's spy.

One fine day, a month after my reports, when I was going through the worst of my periods and had insisted the previous night that I would stay over at my place and not her home, the doorbell rang at seven in the morning.

I was barely able to get out of bed. Not being one to have guests at home, and definitely not at seven in the morning, I opened the door and to my astonishment, there stood my dad.

'I am having none of your nonsense, *bete*. I have got the car. We are packing your stuff and we are heading home.'

Yep. That was his opening sentence. No preamble. No nonsense. Straight to the point. That's my dad for you.

'I can't just pack up and leave! I am not leaving my job!'

Yep. That was me. Hysterical, confused, pain momentarily forgotten, comically shouting at the gate that opened right onto the street.

'You can find another job when you are in a position to do one. I will be waiting at *Bua's*, just come up to her place.'

Waiting at *Bua's*. He was waiting at my aunt's place. And just like that, I was uprooted and moved away.

Imagine having your dream job, heading a team of twenty people one day, and the next, simply being plucked out of that life like a helpless rose in full bloom. I gave in my notice in the most historically unprofessional way, over a call, telling my boss that I had already left and that I would be back at a later date to finish the backlog.

It was a six-hour journey from Delhi to home and I spoke not a single word.

Everything that I had worked so hard to carefully build had come crashing down. We reached my parent's house and I withdrew from everything. I was a disaster waiting to happen. It was as if my body gave up whatever resistance it had the moment we reached home. I couldn't hold myself up, and my intensive treatment began almost the very next day.

Fast forward six months.

I was still nursing the hurt over being snatched away from my life so unceremoniously. I barely talked and what little I said, could never be termed polite.

I had also developed a new pain. A 'lump' had developed somewhere at the back of my neck. It was a dull, persistent pain that I ignored, until it could no longer be avoided.

Another round of scans, another round of medical experts, this time from a new department and another earth-shattering report came my way.

The doctors suspected the lump to be a malicious growth that could turn cancerous.

I had read the expression 'dropped a bomb' a million times before, but in that one moment I understood what it really meant.

I pleaded with the doctors. There had to be some mistake. I didn't drink. I didn't smoke. Heck, my friends tried not to smoke around me.

What could possibly give me cancer?

My career was already down the drain, my pain was not getting any better and here I faced a threat that I couldn't fathom, let alone deal with.

My first surgery was scheduled two days after the report came.

After that, the lump was gone but the pain remained.

I was at one of the lowest points in my life. The only people I really talked to were those in my writing group and my former boss. No, she hadn't disowned me. We had worked out a compromise where I turned in all my backlog within a stipulated timeframe and left my dreams and my career behind for good.

I retreated further into my shell and my family just stood by me, letting me figure out my own coping mechanism.

Two months later, the lump appeared again. It was removed. And a month later, it came back, again.

I generally did not like anybody visiting me at the hospital. I couldn't deal with the people who mattered to me seeing me in those depressing, drab hospital whites.

After my seventh surgery, one of my seniors from my writing group had come to visit.

I refused to see him, but he persisted.

'How have you been doing?' he asked.

I raised my eyebrow, and then stared at him as if to ask, 'What do you think?'

I was in pain, had lost faith in all that was good, and didn't even know if this nightmare would end at all. What was the answer to the question, really?

What had I done to deserve this ordeal?

My family was stuck with a cranky, silent daughter who would not tell them anything. I had not written anything in months and had not been published anywhere. My only solace were the books I read.

There was no reason for me to be cordial.

The person visiting me pulled a chair out and sat next to me, uninvited.

'I talked to your dad,' he said.

'Good, now you don't need to talk to me.' I tried brushing him off.

'You know, you really don't need to say anything. Just hear me out. I am going to tell you a story. You may have heard it before. Or you may not have. Just hear me out till the end, without interrupting,' he said.

I kept staring at him.

He began.

'Eons ago, in the times when the gods walked the Earth, and the human sages had open access to the gods, the king of gods, Indra was blessed by the most reputed sage of all times, *Rishi* Durvasa. As a blessing, *Rishi* Durvasa gave Indra a garland that

Indra put around his elephant's neck before leaving for heaven. Now, on the way, the fragrance from the garland became too overwhelming for the poor elephant. He shook it off his neck and the garland landed on the floor.

'When Durvasa saw this, he was livid. He cursed Indra for rejecting his gift and insulting him. As a result, Indra would be stripped of all his riches.

'Durvasa returned to his hermitage and sure enough, the entire heaven emptied out. All the gods were stripped of their riches and the goddess of wealth, Lakshmi, retreated deep into the eternal sea of Ksheer-Sagara. Since the goddess Lakshmi vanished, wealth and fertility vanished not only from heaven, but also from earth and the demon realms.

'It was an apocalyptic situation.

'The solution to this grave problem would come from the Holy Trinity. Lord Vishnu, the second of the Holy Trinity, advised that in order for wealth to come back to the world, the eternal sea would have to be churned.

'To agitate a body of water as huge as the sea, there needed to be a churner of adequate magnitude. The mountain, Mandranchal Giri, was kindly requested to rise up to the occasion and he complied. The snake servant to Lord Vishnu, Vasuki became the rope. Lord Vishnu himself took the form of a tortoise called Kurma to stabilise the mountain on his back. Once the Mandrachal Giri was firmly placed on Kurma's back, the head side of the serpent Vasuki was held by the demons and the tail end was held by the gods.

'Thus, began the churning of the sea by gods and demons.

'After ages and ages of churning, the sea finally started yielding fruit. But what came out horrified the gods, the demons and the Holy Trinity.'

I was listening in rapt attention. I had heard the story before, but there was something in the way that he told it, that I was transfixed. I had a feeling this was going somewhere.

'You know what came out first? The *halaahala*. The poison. Deadlier than any poison ever produced or would ever be produced in the universe. The sea had placed a condition, that for the remaining fruits of the sea to come out, the previous one had to be consumed.

'Someone had to consume this poison first. This poison was so deadly, that even the Holy Trinity wouldn't survive it. It was then, that Lord Shiva, the third of the Holy Trinity, took the pot in his hands and sat down by the seaside. He started drinking from the pot, but his consort goddess Parvati placed her hands tightly around his throat and didn't let the poison slip down his throat.

'The poison was consumed.

'Then out came the goddess Lakshmi from the sea, bearing riches, fertility and medicinal sciences the like of which had never been seen before.'

He stopped to take a deep breath.

'I know this. My *nani* has narrated this to me so many times.' I told him, but the bite had gone out of my voice. There is something about the stories of your childhood, especially the ones told by grandmothers – they have the charm to soothe an aching heart.

‘You are not getting the point here, Vri. It’s the poison. For any good to come along, the sea has to be churned. The poison, the *halaahala* has to be thrown out. This suffering of yours my dear, is your *halaahala*. You might not be able to write today, but you will surely write about this someday. You are churning yourself. This suffering, this bitterness – it will all go away, and then what will come is going to be pure bliss. Bear this small portion of *halaahala*, will you now, my sister?’

I leapt out of the bed and hugged him. Of the many things that I had done over the past several months, one thing I had not done was cried. But that evening I cried and cried till I emptied myself out onto his shoulder.

He held me as a dear elder brother would.

He who came from a different culture, different mother, and different language, had bound me to him by a shared story that had been passed down to us as a heritage, and a simple understanding that life itself had become poison for me.

I underwent two more surgeries after that. But neither of them were able to embitter me again.

All this had given me a lot of time to think about myself. My work that had come to an abrupt halt needed a jump start and I realised I needed work to remain sane. My family was the rock that anchored me and the soil that did not let me wither away, but they wouldn’t let me start working again.

I had a father who was worried, as all Indian fathers do, about his only daughter's wedding. I am, by all Indian standards, over the normal marriageable age. My parents didn't let it show, but I knew there was so much eating at them.

I had lost enough, to PCOS, to cancer threats, to circumstances.

Again, I called up my boss. She said, 'You know I love you to death girl, but I can't support you on this decision. I am with your family on this.'

I told her that this did not sit well with me. That it had been more than year that I had been at home, and frankly, I wanted my life back.

'You need a fresh perspective, maybe a break.' After a little thought she said, 'Why don't you apply for a Master's of Publishing?'

Her experience shone through her advice and the idea stuck.

I called my professors from back in my post-graduate school, my mentor from my writing group, my former editors at the newspaper I worked at, and all of them were in favour. It seemed perfect.

Then came the first hurdle: my father did not agree.

He was too scared to let me out of his sight. He had almost lost his daughter and did not have it in him to send her away.

I could never have expected what happened after that. My father received call after call from people convincing him to let me go.

My professors, my writing mentor, my boss, my writing

group, the brother that had visited me in hospital, even my doctor, all called him up, giving him different reasons as to why going overseas was just what I needed.

I found support in people who had just met me in literature festivals. Some connected me to their friends in Sydney, so it wouldn't be lonely for me, and some connected me to relatives who I could visit occasionally.

Even my cousins who live in Australia put my case to my father. They accepted complete responsibility for me, even though they live in a different city. I am fortunate to have them.

My father finally understood my desire to study more and agreed.

It was then that I realised, it wasn't just my grit or passion that had got me this far. It was love. Love and support that flowed from different people absolutely unrelated to each other, who could have just walked away from me, but they didn't.

They stood by me. I had always heard that it takes a village to raise a child. But what no one says is, it takes an empathetic community for an adult to thrive. When they came together to hold me, they did not see my religion, my colour, my origin or even my abrupt departure. All they saw was a girl, who had had enough and who needed their love and support.

I had so many hands keeping me from falling apart, and you couldn't tell one from another. Or maybe you could, but that just makes it more beautiful.

Together they, the multi-coloured stones of my road to Australia paved a way for me to connect to my dreams again. If I could take flight to my dreams again, it was because so many people became the wind beneath my wings.

I never thanked them. I don't think a thank you justifies what they did for me.

I'd rather pay it forward.

That is how we overcome differences, that is how we keep love flowing. A single moment of empathy during someone else's lowest point makes them a better human, and in that process creates a better world.

I still have a lot of *halaahala* to churn out, but the beauty that I received then, and keep receiving here in Sydney, makes it worth all the pain.

This journey has taught me, and continues to teach me the power of gratitude, love and empathy.

IRAN

Raz Badiyan

Iran, you feel like a dream.
Not because of how magical you are
for which, regarding your past
for one second, I do not doubt.

You are a dream because you are too far
both in distance and in heart,
and I struggle to be free
knowing that all my life you have been calling me.
I leave your messages on seen
with no intention of replying.

And, as much as I want to forgive,
I wanted to let you know

Iran, I love you,

so, I've decided to let you go.

STARRY NIGHT

Naosheyrvaan Nasir

There is nothing quite like a starry night
Meteors racing through the dark sky,
A disco party of lights.

A blanket of darkness blinds us all
A mathematical compass guides you
A polka dot pattern, custom designed
A disease, virtually unstoppable
Madly holding onto the horizon.

An impressionist work by Van Gogh
Stars of different colours, shapes and sizes
Each with their own magical properties
All the cool kids clustered in the middle
While the lonely ones scatter all over the place.
An unforgettable experience.

TREE OF LIFE

Scott Whittingham

Spread thy wings,
Through times of gale
The harshness and beauty of nature,
Also reveal splendour.

Like leaves we may become detached,
Fall, flutter and be taken away from the tree
Without this detachment,
There cannot be nourishment.

To touch a falling leaf,
That shimmers and descends with a vibrancy of colour
Like the rings of a tree,
We have times of plentiful engagement.

Nourishment arises in various forms
Of psychological, spiritual, and embodied perspectives.

The warmth of the autumn sun,
In contrast to the icy mountain breeze –
Positive states of mind fluctuate with cyclical seasons

We move forward in the warmth,
Planning for the winter like a bird
Perched upon a leafless tree,
Resting for the journey beyond.

Like a Snowy Mountain pygmy possum
Awakening from a deep torpor,
We emerge from the darkness within

The heart beats ever so slowly
Life-giving warmth gradually melts,
Dissipating snow in the comfort of new frontiers

The journey beyond the darkness of self-enclosure,
Emerges like a clinging cicada,
Crawling upwards to the sun

Awaiting seeds emerge on the sacred Earth
Amid Mother Nature's unpredictability,
Within the construct of time,
And the ever-expanding universe
We attempt to move beyond physical constraints,
To a place where renewal and positive energy may result.

REMEMBERING EUNICE

Gabrielle Cadenhead

He huddles, fragile limbs
masking loud tears,
cradling this stick-brittle husk
of the person he wants to be.

He bares his child bones,
reaching back to a rose tinted past
of wooden bedrooms
and red print carpet.

Bones which disintegrated
by his grandmother's deathbed
as she whispered secret words
with stolen breath.

His brittle cartilage collapses
in my arms and he becomes
a pile of memories.

Nothing was left unscathed:
the flames claimed
her leather armchair
and vintage kitchen,
and cleaved the house in two.

Lives were not lost
but the blaze shortened hers;
a scented candle
decimated family heirlooms.

He is broken, and I
cannot unbreak him.
Child bones curve inwards –
they dare not grow beyond her memory,
desperate to preserve a hint of rose
amid the flames.

We are a pile of bones,
cheeks plastered with shared tears,
our future the ashes of memory.

PLANT AND ANIMAL

Elizabeth Mora

My grandmother, her memory, was a seed that bloomed in someone else's garden. This is a truth reluctantly expressed with the grief of not being able to prevent it. My grandmother's last wish was to rest in peace, to see fulfilled the expectation that I, her granddaughter, would find mine. 'I leave the world I brought you into,' said a letter found inside the casing of her jewellery box. 'Keep me close enough to see it has treated you better than me.' These words are not mere poeticism; they recall a very well-known tradition.

In pre-Columbian times, South America was ruled by a tribe that the Spanish explorer Francisco Orellana later called the Amazonian matriarchy. The tribe believed they had been sent by Venus, the goddess of fertility, to share a symbiotic relationship with the Earth. The energy that flowed through their veins ushered them towards keeping the Earth's reproduction cycles in sync with one another. Landforms, animals and plants would, under their guidance, multiply, evolve and diversify.

Mama Agua, the original caregiver of life on Earth, seeing the fruits of their labour, would become their ally, offering herself willingly to their project of growth and preservation. Along with this, in return for their duties on Earth, she would grant their descendants three lives. The first, the story of creation, was a life guaranteed. The parable of the lost daughter, a story about retrospective insight, would inspire the lessons of the second. And the third would be a celebration of life itself. This life cycle was sometimes called the Song of Peace or Life Everlasting. Whether their descendants reached their second and third life depended on the guidance granted to them as they confronted and adapted to the complexities that arose in newer times and places.

***

In the time of the Amazonian matriarchy, it was believed that womanliness was an essence that first emerged in the natural world. The first woman of their tribe was not human; she was made from a hungry volcano that had eaten three meteorites. One would become her mind, another, her body, and the last, her heart. Many centuries ago, pieces of extra-terrestrial debris from Venus strayed from their orbits in outer space and caught in Earth's gravity. As they neared the Earth's surface, friction in the air transformed these particles into an enchanting incandescent performance; a thick row of shooting stars cascading downward, in search of their destiny. The ones that survived the flight through the Earth's atmosphere were believed to have fallen onto the foam margins of the Napo River, a large river mouth in charge of singing lullabies that would keep dormant volcanoes asleep.

The impact of their landing made the Earth shake. Sensing that these foreign guests might try to entertain her neighbours out of sleep, the Napo River sang louder and for longer than usual. All returned to their slumber, except one.

Cotopaxi was a crater that formed part of the shoreline on which these stars had fallen. The radiance of these tiny firecrackers, still sizzling from the scars of their audacious escapade, fascinated her. They reminded her of the days she too was a plume of light writing her own destiny, in the opposite direction. They smelled good too; it was a metallic temptation so similar to the burnt silver that decorated the ovoid bodies of the freshwater piranhas that the Napo River poured into her belly during rainstorms. She watched as they danced on the edges of her mouth, bouncing up and down the cushions of her lips like a freedom dance. She turned to the Napo River, paused for a moment, then swallowed.

It was believed that all women of the tribe were created in similar circumstances: by interrupting, inheriting and sustaining the dreams of a variety of landforms, as well as communities of fauna and flora. Like Cotopaxi, some women roamed the Earth in the skin of vast terrestrial landscapes, adding distinct shapes to its surface. Some were as steadfast as mountains. Some were as white as the Patagonian ice fields. Other Venus sisters had acquired the strength and velocity of the animal world. She might have been seen flying in the disguise of the Harpy eagle or marking the hunting trail of the elusive Puma.

My grandmother was Mujer Orquídea, a late descendant of the Venus sister that had inherited the care of the largest family of plants in the entire world: the orchid. She was a self-sufficient flower that could survive days without water. Being an epiphyte, she was rootless and agile, and could often be spotted in the Amazonian forest, climbing towards the top of tall canopies for a generous dose of sunlight.

One day, Mujer Orquídea made a life-changing mistake. After weeks spent at the top of the canopy, she was overcome by heatstroke. Her body, already weak from dehydration, struggled miserably to hold onto the trunks and vines elevating her. Soon, she found herself plummeting without constraint towards the ground. On the forest floor, walking straight under my grandmother's downfall, was Hombre Ego. He was a hairless, barebacked Homo Sapien – a late descendant of the Mars brother who had inherited the care of the Hominidae family.

When Mujer Orquídea fell onto his right arm, sliding effortlessly down his shoulder, up, over and down his firm biceps, and into the soft palm of his hand, my grandmother thought her first life on Earth would soon end. She didn't mind. The animal would eat her and nourish itself; it was part of the cycle of life. She was wrong. This creature was not hungry; he was a curious loner who had been roaming the forest in search of trouble.

'Are you dying?'

'Yes. If *Mama Agua* doesn't help me soon ... '

'Who is *Mama Agua*?'

'The rivers, lakes, oceans, the springs ... '

'Oh, you need water, I can fix that.'

'No, you need to ask first ... '

'No I don't. I have all the water in the world.'

'But that's impossible! If you have all the water in the world then ... '

'Where I come from,' he'd interrupted, 'we do not ask permission for anything. We take what we need and that's that.'

At this point, he had leaned onto his back leg, turned his left arm into a side triangle that rested on his left waist, pushed his shoulders back, accentuating as he did, the outward curve of his chest, and moving his right nipple closer to the palm in which my grandmother languished. It had stared at her straight in the eyes. My grandmother had stared back, surprised at how freely it offered itself for observation.

'Has anyone told you how beautiful you are?'

'Beautiful?'

My grandmother had looked up at his mouth; distracted by the sound of a word she had always heard sparingly, consciously.

'Yes. You are very, very ... '

***

This is how Mujer Orquídea, my grandmother, ended up far away from home, in the city of Cuenca, Ecuador. Here, she lived in a green baroque style house that reminded her of a suffocated garden. Vines, orchids and other plants were wrapped around the necks of concrete pillars like gold necklaces, trapped inside ceramic wombs and rooted in tight soil-filled squares bordered by bricks and wooden fences. Unable to leave, she was coerced into a life of servitude. She would spend most of her first life, the one designated to constructing oneself, cleaning white walls and pushing against the body of a man who had already broken hers. When Hombre Ego's wife found out Mujer Orquídea was pregnant, she offered her a premonitory gesture of goodwill that would haunt her till her death. In her hands she had placed the equivalent of a year's worth of savings and told her, '*Mi casa* is not the place for a second life.'

Second life?

This child would be her second life?

What of the parable of the lost daughter?

Would her daughter be condemned to a life of redemption?

Was *Mama Agua* trying to punish her for leaving the tribe?

***

My mother grew up unaware of her destiny. My grandmother had thought that if she avoided it, it couldn't affect how her daughter saw herself and her place in the world. *My daughter will not be used by Mama Agua to teach me a lesson,* she had thought. Instead, she hoped her daughter would carve out a new identity in the Patriarchy, the original name of the city to which

Hombre Ego had brought her. There she would educate herself into the ways of this tribe and it would, in turn, treat her as one of their own; as an equal.

Unfortunately, this was an idealism inherited from her days with the Amazonian matriarchy. When everyone and anyone that worked hard was rewarded with a place in the community. My mother remembered feeling lost and alone. Like the hero of an unwritten story. Unable to diagnose her mother's silence to recurring questions about her heritage:

Why do people say I am the daughter of a flower?

Is it true?

Why then is my skin green?

Why do gardens grow in secret places?

Why does the river song sound like a woman crying?

She decided to search out her father and ask him. She located him but never really found him. In the place of her father, a figure she had dreamed about ever since she had noticed other girls idolise theirs, she found the knife of my grandmother's pain, *the one she had intentionally erased from her life*. She found a man irreversibly conditioned by the permanency of having travelled beyond reason.

***

'I will make him rot for this,' Mujer Orquídea had decreed, clenching her right fist and motioning it towards the giant globe growing underneath her daughter's breasts. In response, my mother, bedridden and sore, had turned her head defiantly towards the only window in the rickety room my grandmother rented since her eviction from Hombre Ego's mansion. Feeling a tidal wave of hot tears surge up her throat and peak on the edge of her eyelids, she had closed them shut, tightened her lips and breathed in heavily.

'*Como va ser*. How can it be,' my grandmother had pleaded, 'this isn't how things – '

'*Por favour* Mama! Please Mama! Please stop!' My mother had interrupted, her eyes still sealed, her head still turned away from her mother's gaze as her right hand, vertically drawn, cut through each of her mother's words, mercilessly.

Mujer Orquídea had been repeating this scene, every Sunday, for nine months, with the same wallowing and unrestrained grief that only a mother can understand. Over time she had learnt to act out her soliloquy like a flawed anti-hero praying to be absolved of her fate. That particular Sunday, as the feverish energy of her unfinished lines spoke through her hands like the wings of a condor in full flight, she had walked in tight circles around her daughter's bed mapping the revenge with which she would reclaim her and her daughter's honour.

At first my mother had thought grandmother was performing an Andean translation of what you might call an exorcism. But before any unwanted spirits could be evicted, she'd made herself dizzy. After the ninth cycle her small frame had begun to sway, the unsteadiness took hold and soon her body fell onto the bed at the end of my mother's swollen feet. Against the squeaky orchestra of old mattress springs expanding and contracting, an unbroken stream of tears had erupted from within her as if on cue. The push and pull of repressed sorrow, heard in the rise of faint whimpers through an air heavy enough to suppress their release, decorated her fragility with a poetic sentimentality.

Sensing her mother's reluctant surrender, my mother had opened her eyes and let the blue swell cascade over her face. She had leaned forward and cupped the amnesty on her mother's face. The fact that this Sunday could have been just like any other Sunday had suddenly dawned on Mujer Orquídea.

She had looked up at her daughter, wiped her tears with her sleeve, turned sideways and silently stared at her womb. As she let her hand climb this manmade summit, she felt her body reverberate the silent roar of a pain she too had once felt.

***

Days before I was born, grandmother tried to return to the Amazonian forest. After many years of trying to avoid it, she would finally confront her pride and ask *Mama Agua* for forgiveness. Overwhelmed by the subtlety of her daughter's strength, she had left the room singing the song of her newfound peace:

Forgive me for thinking that your intention was against me.
Forgive me for not listening, for believing I knew better.

Forgive me for trying to heal pain with pain.
Thank you for my daughter.
Thank you for sharing a wisdom that transcends.
Thank you for a love that is endless.

May my granddaughter live on and on and on.
I leave the world I brought you into.
When I return, and I will, keep me close enough to see.
May this world treat you better than it treated me.

ABOUT THE CONTRIBUTORS

Memi Adams

'Oak Tree' and 'Pine Tree' are ink and charcoal illustrations. I chose these mediums to convey the unique characteristics of both trees. I have a collection of works that are primarily inspired by nature, as I believe flora and fauna are rich representations of the beauty of diversity. Further, these illustrations were made to communicate a greater message, which is the value of biodiversity. As plant and wildlife diversity is necessary for a thriving ecosystem, similarly each life has a purpose that is unique and individual to the person. Hence, as we preserve the Earth's biodiversity, we can also learn to see the importance of diversity and inclusion in our communities.

Sofia Ahmad

'Young girl struggling with identity; drowns feelings by baking (very badly), listening to classic rock, and – occasionally – writing a thing or two.' I'm a reader who accidentally started writing and somehow, the cogs clicked and fell right into place. Though my heart lies in the fantasy genre, my poetry usually explores subjects more personal to me. In 'Ecotone', I explore the disjointed terrain between my Pakistani heritage and Australian upbringing, celebrating the mismatched identity I've learned to form out of both. You can find more of me at: sofiaswritings.poetry.blog

Misbah Ansari

I am an eighteen-year-old Arts/Law student at the University of Sydney. I like to talk about gender, Harry Potter, emotions, poetry, and everything in between. My works have been previously published in *The Bombay Review*, *Coldnoon*, *The Hindu*, *Feminism in India*, *LiveWire* and other such platforms. I hail from Mumbai, India, and my upbringing and cultural experiences have formed an integral part of my literary journey. I want to see more people getting engaged with Indian literature and want to bring it to the mainstream media.

Mohammad Awad

I am a Health and Psychology student working in mental health, striving to destigmatise mental health in diverse communities. A writer/artist/musician/poet who's running out of ways to express myself.

Published in an anthology series 'Arab, Australian, Other' among writers such as Sara Saleh and Randa Abdel-Fattah, I have been featured in *The Daily Telegraph*, *Honi-Soit* magazine, and have been a Bankstown Poetry Grand Slam finalist for three consecutive years. I was a NSW State finalist in 2019's Australian Poetry Slam, taking first place in the Western Sydney finals. I have also featured for Word in Hand, White Ribbon events and Project Opinions, in addition to being featured on *SBS Radio*, *Eastside Radio*, *2SER* and *FBI Radio*.

I work as the youngest Peer Worker and Mental Health Worker in NSW Health history, conducting lectures at the University of Sydney on the importance of lived experience in recovery-oriented practice and develop poetry therapy groups for acute mental health facilities in the state.

Raz Badiyan

I am a lover, desiring to express it all in words. I have been writing poetry and prose since I was seven years of age. I am emotionally influenced by people, conversations and (mainly) the ocean. I am currently working on publishing my first collection of poetry. You can find and follow my work @rbwords on Instagram.

Gabrielle Cadenhead

I am a writer, composer and flautist interested in the intersection between my artforms, as well as the symbiosis of creativity, activism and faith. I curate new music performances with Konzertprojekt, and my fiction and poetry have been published in *ARNA*. gabriellecadenhead.wixsite.com/gabriellecadenhead

Jing Cai

It was a joyful experience to write something from the heart for the anthology, and share it with someone who may resonate. As a current PhD candidate at the Sydney Conservatorium of Music, and a previous opera project manager and television programme director, writing has always been an important part of my life, though for different objectives and readers. With my pen, I hope to write more stories about opera, art and culture for the past, the present and the future.

Bethany Carter

I hold a Bachelor of Education, a Bachelor of Social Science (Psychology) and Diploma of Music, and I am currently undertaking a Master of Music (Music Education). I have over ten years' teaching and performing experience on harp (pedal and Celtic) and piano. I have been involved in choral ensembles as a singer and conductor, and I am concert band and string ensemble conductor and English teacher at a secondary school in the Central West. I am regularly involved in community theatrical productions both as an instrumentalist and cast member, and particularly enjoy contributing musically to fundraisers and other community events.

Adelia Croser

I am a publishing student, who's hoping this is her final career choice, after getting lost in a law degree for too many years. I don't normally consider myself a writer but appreciate the way it can allow us to explore issues that we wouldn't usually confront and work through them at our own pace. In the year I've been studying at the University of Sydney, I've learned to love the small quiet spaces (no, I won't tell you where they are) and hate the people who chase you down with flyers on Eastern Avenue. I still haven't figured out when any of the cafes on campus close by, but by god do I have an opinion on who makes the best coffee (it's Manning Kiosk and you know it).

Keesha Field

I am a second-year university student of a Bachelor of Visual Art and Advanced Studies at Sydney College of the Arts. I am largely concerned with the human form – my interest unwavering despite my multidisciplinary practice. I am fascinated by the innate similarities all humans have despite perceived differences and seek to celebrate this fact through my video work, 'Elle Est L'Univers' (2019). My work features the female body where the anonymity of the subject is a sentiment to all women and anyone who identifies as such.

Lou Garcia-Dolnik

I am a writer, editor and harpist working at the intersection of gender, sexuality and place. Living on unceded Gadigal land,

I am the editor of *Hermes*, the University of Sydney Union's annual creative catalogue and Australia's oldest literary journal, and the prose team leader for the journal *ARNA*. A participant in Express Media's Toolkits: Poetry program, I have work in and forthcoming with Voiceworks.

Katarina Grobler

I am a young Australian pianist, currently in my third year of undergraduate performance studies at the Sydney Conservatorium of Music. A multi-instrumentalist, I also regularly perform on trumpet with the Young Women's Jazz Orchestra and am a member of various chamber groups including Trio Molto Ironico and Ensemble Muse, all of which have a focus on performing Australian and/or twenty-first-century repertoire. I am also extremely interested in cultural studies and in research surrounding the subject of gender in musicology and aspire to undertake further research in this area.

John Hannaford

With a full-time role delivering social justice outcomes to marginalised and vulnerable communities, I bring a creative balance to my professional life by volunteering with Sydney Gay and Lesbian Mardi Gras. Since discovering a talent for balancing logistical challenges with artistic expression, I have proudly worked alongside the dedicated team that produces the Mardi Gras Parade each year. During those few moments when I am not juggling work commitments or parade planning, I am engaged in part-time postgraduate study at the University of Sydney.

Djuna Hallsworth

I am a third-year PhD candidate in the Department of Gender and Cultural Studies, researching the representation of women in Danish film and television. In addition to my love of foreign and indie films, I am curious about the way the camera captures moving images into still frames. Photography is a hobby I have taken up recently, and one that I enjoy because of the way it encourages me to interact differently with my environment.

Sarah Carol Hughes

I am a writer and stage manager from southern California, where I received a Bachelor of Arts in Theatre. I am currently a postgraduate student at the University of Sydney studying a Master of Creative Writing. I write about travel and all things science fiction.

Vrishali Jain

Donning many hats as a writer, editor, journalist, social media strategist, cashier, a company secretary aspirant (thankfully not seeing this one through), I found home in publishing. Pursuing a Master's degree in Publishing at the University of Sydney, volunteering for various social campaigns as a Student Representative of the Faculty of Arts and Social Sciences, and writing radio stories for various channels in India defines my current life largely. I can generally be spotted at various libraries across the university campus with a can of coke (I know, not very healthy) or a cup of coffee (arguably unhealthy again). Heading for my last semester at the university, I am now hoping to carve my own dusty trail into the publishing industry.

Grace Jing Johnson

I'm a current piano performance student at the Sydney Conservatorium of Music. Since being at Sydney Uni, I have written extensively for *Honi Soit* and have also contributed to *Pulp* and *CutCommon* classical music magazine, as well as the 2018 student anthology.

Harold Legaspi

I am a Sydney-based poet, novelist, writer of short fiction and essayist who migrated to Australia from the Philippines in 1989. My writing has been published in Australia and abroad. I am the founding editor of *Lite Lit One*, a bi-annual online journal of fiction and poetry. My book, *Letters in Language*, was the runner-up in the 2019 Puncher & Wattmann Prize for a First Book of Poetry.

Maeve Marsden

I am a writer, performer, producer and director. I curate *Queerstories*, a national storytelling project comprised of live events, an award-winning podcast and a collection of stories I edited and were published by Hachette.

As a well-respected cultural commentator, I have hosted events for Sydney Writer's Festival, Mudgee Readers' Festival, Newcastle Writers Festival, Adelaide Writers Week and Ubud Writers and Readers Festival. I also curate Queer Thinking, Sydney Mardi Gras' two-day talks and ideas festival. I have been published by *The Sydney Morning Herald*, *Guardian Australia*, *Junkee*, *ABC*, *SBS*, *ArtsHub*, *Daily Review*, *Archer Magazine* and *Audrey Journal*. In 2020, I will be a member of Belvoir Theatre's Philip Parsons Writers Lab for Early-Career Playwrights.

I like gin, dancing, cheese and TV melodramas with good ethics and bad dialogue.

Elizabeth Mora

I am the daughter of two love-struck Ecuadorians. I learnt from a young age to appreciate stories as moments of possibility. Tales of passion, resilience and risks taken valiantly have shaped my worldview and inspired me to search for alternative truths. I am currently studying to become a secondary school teacher. In my spare time, I write and produce ear stories about identity, love and irreconcilable futures. Find me at: thelightthedark.wordpress.com

James Mukheibir

I am a Media and Communications student, majoring in film studies. An avid lover and creator of theatre, I have been an active member of the Sydney University Dramatic Society for the past three years. This story was a painful process and I hope that it helps others interrogate their own place in the world more easily. This is not a piece designed to give answers, but rather to provide more questions, hopefully the right questions to help our world heal.

Rosie Mulray

I am about to finish a Master of Publishing, and occasionally I like to write things in miscellaneous genres when inspiration strikes. I am a freelance copy editor and proofreader, specialising in academic manuscripts, hoping to make my way into the Sydney publishing industry after graduating.

Naosheyrvaan Nasir

A proud resident of Western Sydney – as USyd rarely has anyone from out west – I have completed my first year of a double degree in Economics and Project Management. I was inspired by my year nine English teacher to take up writing, and in year twelve, I won the poetry section at my school's inaugural spring writing competition. I have written a variety of text types (beyond the essays and narratives for the HSC) such as letters to the editor, speeches, blogs, and diary entries. I spend my free time volunteering at my mosque (in Marsden Park), annoying my siblings and making my Twitter presence known through @nao_nasir.

Rhea L Nath

I am a freelance writer, editor, and content creator. Although I reside in Sydney, I consider myself a Bangalore girl at heart. My poetry has been previously featured in *Hakara Journal*, *Cogito – The Literary Journal*, and *Oddball Magazine* and I hope to get started on a series of young adult novels ... eventually.

Connor Parissis

As a Queer activist and writer, I write for a world that otherwise seeks to silence us. In 2017 I served as the University of Sydney Queer Officer and in 2019 ran as a federal candidate for the Greens. I currently study a Master of Publishing whilst fretting over climate change and the amount of books in my 'to-read' pile.

Sarah Poh

I speak more in my writing than in person. Though my poetry and prose have been published in a few anthologies, I am more a reader than a writer. I also drink tea as if it's water and watch one too many cooking videos.

Yasodara S.B.W. Puhule-Gamayalage

I am a Bachelor of Arts (Media and Communications) (Hons) student with an amateur zeal for visual arts and minimal music. The issue of colourism has become a significant part of my current exploration of the erosion of the subaltern self at the face of intra-cultural prejudices.

Hannah Roux

My family moved to Australia ten years ago when I was ten years old. These poems mark some sense of dislocation in the Australian landscapes and seasons, which are so difficult to fit into traditional ideas of spring, summer, autumn and winter. Seasonal dislocation here also stands in for cultural difference, and the difficulty of imposing English, a foreign language bred in a foreign land, on the Australian landscape.

Mary Stanley

I am a speculative fiction writer and freelance editor from the Illawarra and am studying publishing at the University of Sydney. I juggle numerous projects at a time and am heavily involved in the Wollongong theatre community. Stories that challenge moral standing and explore the disturbing intimacies of strained relationships have always intrigued me, and this led me to write 'Assimilation'. My piece aims to demonstrate that sometimes, against our own hopes and efforts, there is no easy fix to tensions around diversity and discrimination. We might be lost today, but how will we make tomorrow different?

Sheree Strange

I am a writer living and working on Gadigal land. I have had work published in *Going Down Swinging*, *Apocalips*, and Better Read Than Dead's *Winter Writing* anthology. I review literature of all kinds for my blog, *Keeping Up With The Penguins*, and I am studying creative writing at the University of Sydney.

Anastasia Taig

I am a research student in the Discipline of Work and Organisational Studies at the University of Sydney Business School. Over the years, poetry has provided me with an escape, an outlet for the challenges of growing older, and a way of exploring the human experience. I love the raw, bloody and beautiful way in which words can capture our lives. I particularly admire the work of Carol Ann Duffy and Mary Oliver.

Amy Wang

I am a third-year science student majoring in psychology. My writing mostly draws upon my experiences with mental illness and daily encounters as a young Chinese/Korean Australian woman.

Ivy Waters

I am a student of philosophy and biological sciences who has been writing fiction in some form or another for the last decade. Currently, I am theoretically working on my novel, when I'm not participating in short fiction competitions, writing fanfiction and philosophy essays, or working on my other novel. I write in just about any genre I can get my hands on, preferably while on public transport, listening to whatever music I'm currently obsessed with, and trying to ignore my other responsibilities.

Elizabeth Wheeler (ATLAS)

I am an international student from Northeastern University, Boston MA, USA. I love to experiment with style, technique and subject in writing, as is obvious in 'Dinner in the Underground', with its ambiguously awkward narrator. I have previously been published in the *Silent Voices* anthology and I am a winner of a Gold Key for poetry and Silver Key for portfolio in the Scholastic Writing Awards. You can find more about me on Instagram, @atlas.write.

Scott Whittingham

My poetry is associated with genetic, human, psychological and environmental diversity. I often associate my paintings and artwork with my poetry and see myself as an emerging artist and writer. I plan to engage with fiction and non-fiction writing in the future along with my visual arts practice. Embodiment and its subsequent recollections within the landscape is an occurring theme in my work that aligns with the philosophies of existential phenomenology.

I have been writing poetry since moving to Wollongong in the nineties and have subsequently moved around in various areas of NSW, ranging from the Northern Rivers to the escarpments of the Blue Mountains National Park. My poetry touches on one such instance of the abundance of bird life I have delightfully observed and contextualised within the diversity of varying ecosystems.

Zhipei Zheng

I am a Chinese Australian who moved to live permanently in Australia at a very young age. Growing up in Australia, I had the wonderful opportunity to really immerse myself in the Australian identity. I was able to meet a plethora of people of different cultural backgrounds, which really allowed me to appreciate the importance of diversity and multiculturalism in Australia.

Cherita Zhu

I am twenty-one and I am studying a Bachelor of Commerce (Liberal Studies) at the University of Sydney. I am an editorial model at Chic Model Management, Sydney. My favourite shoes are the black pointy croc-leather heels I am wearing while writing this biography and the sly-eyed J. Barrett is the professional model who inspires me, and if I were to have a pet, I would have a lovely pet bird. I am also a consulting sector cadet at PwC and spend my chill time socialising in starry tall night scenes. Right now I am working on finalising blogs on my life@21: www.ablackheartearring.com X www.astepinkind.com (brb university studies first! Always-!). Love always and enjoy, Miss Cherita Zhu.

ABOUT THE EDITORS

Adelia Croser

I've long been an advocate for diversity in our media, whether it's TV, books or podcasts. It's incredibly important to support people in telling their own stories, and it's been a privilege to be a part of this anthology, whose aim this year has been just that. I can only hope that as I get more experience in the industry, it allows me to support these voices even further. When I'm not doing that, you can find me playing an inordinate amount of Dungeons & Dragons, trying to figure out how to make perfect macarons, or working on the latest subversive cross-stitch project.

Vrishali Jain

I am Vrishali Jain, Vri to all my friends here in Australia. I write one third of the time and think about writing for the rest. Currently pursuing my second Master's degree at the University of Sydney, I have donned many hats, from journalist to writer, social media manager and editor. I have a colourful background with a bachelors in commerce and a previous masters in journalism. I dive into an existential crisis when it comes to editing in no time. Clumsy and kind, I will feed anyone, even at midnight. If I'm not reading, I'm wandering around and emptying coffee shops in town. If you're reading this, forget everything and see me in person. I don't bite but might possibly drive you insane.

Rosie Mulray

I'm an editor and proofreader who specialises in academic copy. I have a background in medical science and theoretical philosophy and have a special affinity for crafting gratifying endings to papers and chapters. In 2020, I'll be looking for more professional projects to expand upon my current publishing industry experience and build my career as an editor. As well as an obvious love of reading and books, I'm happiest when I'm learning something new.

This probably accounts for my love of academic writing, as well as a strange list of hobbies: skating and roller derby, knitting and fibre crafts, practising various musical instruments, listening to the people who can play them properly, collecting teacups and I have a tendency to go on long YouTube journeys learning about new skills and crafts. Oh, and occasionally I write angsty romantic ballads for anthologies.

Emily Smith

Skincare specialist by day, academic proofreader and copy editor by night, I'm a lifelong learner and am currently working on a way to make student life a profession. When I first left school, I struggled to find my academic pathway. Having dipped my toes into first-year medical, teaching, and music degrees, I finally decided on linguistics and literature and found where I thrived.

Honestly, I should have just started with the arts, and I've spent years learning about things I'll never need, but I will absolutely nail every pub trivia night and you bet I'm a queen at crossword puzzles. I have an affinity for science fiction novels, an obsession with Skyrim and I grow tomatoes and beetroot in my balcony's sunshine.

Melissa Snook

I am a lover of books and reading, stuck working in retail. I love all subgenres of young adult, particularly fantasy, and don't tend to read outside the genre (although I do enjoy a good non-fiction book on American politics). My favourite place to read them is either in my armchair in my room, or in my library (decorated in a cross between the Gryffindor common room and BBC Sherlock's living room). When I'm not reading, I'm either gaming, on YouTube or eating good food with my friends. I love playing Final Fantasy XIV and Assassin's Creed, and love watching comedy and baking shows – possibly too much.

Mary Stanley

As a writer and editor, I am dedicated to finding and presenting the raw, emotional core of any story to an audience. Some of my favourite books are *Neuromancer*, *The Road* and *Gone Girl*, and

I am working hard to ensure that my own writing makes as big an impact as these novels had on me.

My short plays have been staged in *Bridge Works*, *24 Hour Theatre* and *Tales from the Metropolis* at the Phoenix Theatre, and my short story *Assimilation* can be found in this anthology. I aim to propel speculative fiction into the literary limelight by writing and publishing stories that everyone can fall in love with.

Jenny Welsh

Originally from Wales, I have lived and worked in France, Germany and the Netherlands and settled in Australia ten years ago. Languages are my passion and I especially enjoy meeting people from different corners of the world. Australia has surprised me with its multiculturalism and diversity, although I believe there is a disconnect between the real Australia and how it is often portrayed in the media, and that is why it is incredibly important to provide a platform for the many distinct voices that make up Australian communities. When I am not studying and running around after my two daughters Bethan and Grace (who love to keep me on my toes with a million questions), I work as a freelance editor at Inner West Editing.

www.ingramcontent.com/pod-product-compliance
Lightning Source LLC
Chambersburg PA
CBHW050843270326
41930CB00020B/3457

* 9 7 8 1 7 4 2 1 0 4 5 7 7 *